nchley Church End Library,
L8 Regents Park Road,
ondon,
? ?LN.

D0335178

30131 05685025 5

LONDON BOROUGH OF BARNET

Praise for *Science(ish)*

'Bright, nerdy and funny! Of course I loved it.'

Dara Ó Briain, writer and comedian

'If you are a geek, a film buff, curious or simply want to know whether you still get BO in space, this is the book you have got to have.'

Kate Humble, BBC TV Presenter

'Deeply funny, academically accomplished, and unfalteringly engaging.'

Ben Miller, comedian and author of *It's Not Rocket Science*

'Explores everything from the ins and outs of black holes (*Interstellar*) to artificial intelligence (*Ex Machina*)... Edwards and Brooks don't take themselves too seriously and their cartoon heads pop up throughout deconstructing the films wittily while explaining the underlying science simply.'

Sunday Times Science Books of the Year

'A terrific, engaging read that brings to life some of the fascinating science that lies behind the movies.'

Johnjoe McFadden, Professor of Genetics, University of Surrey

About the Authors

 Rick Edwards is a writer and television presenter. He is the host of BBC 1's quiz *!mpossible*. Rick has a Natural Sciences degree from Cambridge, which he is finally getting some use out of.

 Dr Michael Brooks is an author, journalist, and consultant for the *New Scientist*. His biggest accomplishment to date is not the PhD in Quantum Physics – it's writing Rick's favourite popular science book, *13 Things That Don't Make Sense*.

Together, they wrote the *Sunday Times* Science Book of the Year, *Science(ish): The Peculiar Science Behind the Movies*. They also present the award-winning podcast *Science(ish)* for Radio Wolfgang. Follow their every move on Twitter @science_ish and the website www.scienceish.org.

Hollywood Wants To Kill You

The Peculiar Science of Death in the Movies

Rick Edwards
Dr Michael Brooks

Atlantic Books
London

First published in hardback in Great Britain in 2019 by Atlantic Books,
an imprint of Atlantic Books Ltd.

Copyright © Rick Edwards and Michael Brooks, 2019

The moral right of Rick Edwards and Michael Brooks to be identified
as the authors of this work has been asserted by them in accordance
with the Copyright, Designs and Patents Act of 1988.

All rights reserved. No part of this publication may be reproduced,
stored in a retrieval system, or transmitted in any form or by any means,
electronic, mechanical, photocopying, recording, or otherwise, without
the prior permission of both the copyright owner and the above
publisher of this book.

1 2 3 4 5 6 7 8 9

A CIP catalogue record for this book is available from
the British Library.

Internal illustrations © www.alternativeaesthetics.co.uk

Hardback ISBN: 978 1 78649 692 8
E-Book ISBN: 978 1 78649 694 2

Printed in Great Britain

Atlantic Books
An Imprint of Atlantic Books Ltd
Ormond House
26–27 Boswell Street
London
WC1N 3JZ

www.atlantic-books.co.uk

Contents

Introduction

This book is for people who can tick the following boxes:

- ☐ I am going to die one day
- ☐ I enjoy watching movies

We should point out straight away that reading this book will probably not prevent your eventual death. There are limits to what you can achieve as an author, even when you're as good at writing as wot we are.

Our goal is a little more modest. We think that, with Hollywood's help, we can improve on who you are. So, if you can tick both boxes, read on.

It may not look like it, but this is a self-help book. We're aware it doesn't have an explicitly self-helpy kind of title. It's not *Six Ways You Can Improve Your Life by Obsessing Over Your Inevitable Demise While Stuffing Yourself with Overpriced Popcorn and Lukewarm Nachos* or *Harness Hollywood and Live Forever (In Your Loved Ones' Hearts)*. But it will make you a better person through our three-step programme:

- Step one: watch some movies. Easy, huh?!
- Step two is almost as easy: read our descriptions of the various ways in which those movies usher in the Grim Reaper.
- Step three is a bit harder: it involves actually facing up to your own death.

1

The good news is, step three is optional. By the time you've completed step two, you'll be a better person anyway. Why? Because, by completing steps one and two, you'll be aware that death is everywhere in the movies. It's not really that Hollywood wants to kill you. It's more that it has no choice. Threatening to kill things is how you get a human being's attention, and your attention is something Hollywood wants very badly.

Every good screenwriter and director knows that something in our programming desires, loves and craves a brush with death. We like to smell the ferrous tang of blood (metaphorically, at least). We thrive on the adrenaline that accompanies the threat. Perversely, it makes us feel alive, and that's what encourages us to be better people and make the most of life.

That's why all human cultures tell stories that revolve around the danger of death. For as long as there has been recorded history and conversation, there have been stories about death. The first recorded story, written on clay tablets 4000 years ago, is a collection of poems known as *The Epic of Gilgamesh*. What's it about? A king's fear of death and his quest for immortality. Some of the most gripping stories written since involve a hero who does battle with a deadly monster: Beowulf vs Grendel, Theseus vs the Minotaur or Rocky vs Ivan Drago.

This human desire for tales that deal with mortality has shaped Hollywood. That's why you'll usually get a brush with death near the beginning of your movie. In *Bambi*, the mother dies (sorry). *Beauty and the Beast*'s Belle has also lost her mother. In fact, so many Disney heroes have lost a parent that it's hard to understand how they ever get their child-friendly ratings. Disney practically has you tripping over wicked stepfathers and evil stepmothers, or caring but incompetent aunts and uncles. From *Frozen* to *Star Wars*, dead relatives launch a shocking number of its plots.

And death is never far away elsewhere in Hollywood, because keeping death close heightens your movie experience. That's why every hero or heroine has to face their own mortality, or deal with an existential threat that looms over them, their family, their community, their planet… maybe even their whole galaxy. Whether they take the form of viruses, sharks, asteroids, homicidal aliens or plain old knife-wielding psychos, death-dealing monsters are always somewhere close by.

It may not sound great, but it is. Partly, because it's an excuse to explore science. Much of scientific endeavour is really about finding ways to avoid death. That's why the pages of this book are filled with the exploits and insights of scientists. They look into outer space to examine the threat from asteroids. They try to work out how to describe death itself – do we mark the cessation of life from when the heart stops beating or when the brain can no longer light up an MRI scanner? How predators evolved, how they kill and how to avoid them have been major scientific themes throughout much of human history. There are very modern questions, too: is our entire species at risk because of artificial hormones released into the environment in modern plastics, for example? Is climate change about to hit a tipping point where our planet is plunged into chaos? Is our current epidemic of sleeplessness going to destroy our minds? And, a century after one of the greatest pandemics of human history, what exactly can we do about the existential threat that viruses create? Are disease and death inevitable, or are we on the cusp of a cure for everything?

In fact, Hollywood's obsession with death is doing us all a favour. For if there's one thing scientists know, it's that a reminder of death makes us get things done. It's the root of most medical advances, for obvious reasons. But it's also the root of agriculture, the construction industry, clothing and all the technologies that started as military innovations. Civilization is, in many ways, a by-product of our uneasy relationship with death.

But it actually goes deeper than that. Various scientific experiments have shown that unapologetic reminders about death make us behave better towards our fellow humans. One study interviewed people about their attitudes to charity and found that people who were standing next to a funeral home during the interview placed a higher value on charitable giving than those interviewed elsewhere. Reminders about death make people reject the pursuit of wealth and fame, and make them focus on the relationships in their lives and becoming a better person.

In fact, made aware of our inevitable death, we strive to form a lasting legacy by creating things like books, or films, or families that will cherish our memory. An experiment that reminded German subjects about their mortality made them more likely to express a desire to have children.

Which is what makes this a self-help book. Dissecting the various ways in which Hollywood wants to kill you – or at least make you contemplate death – will ultimately make you better in every way. Mahatma Gandhi once said, 'Live as if you were to die tomorrow; learn as if you were to live forever.' This book can help you do both.

You're welcome.

Rick and Michael

1

Hollywood Wants to Kill You... WITH A VIRUS!

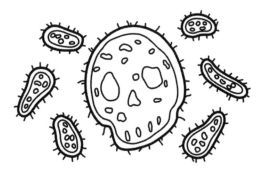

'DON'T TALK TO ANYONE! DON'T TOUCH ANYONE!'

— *Contagion* (2011)

n *Contagion*, a flu-like virus arises in Hong Kong. A visiting American businesswoman becomes infected just before she heads home, and brings the virus with her – to devastating effect. Before long, she and her son are dead, and the authorities responsible for disease control soon realize they are facing a lethal pandemic.

Of the myriad ways in which Hollywood has imagined us dying en masse, the idea of a global pandemic is perhaps the most terrifying. That's because it is one of the most realistic. Global health experts have hailed *Contagion*'s plot as a highly plausible scenario if we're unlucky enough to come up against the wrong virus. Pay attention: this film could save your life.

How Do Viruses Work?

> *Contagion*'s flu is not such a terrible way to die.

> Your lungs get liquefied by a virus. I'm filing that firmly under 'terrible way to die'.

> Hear me out. Every time I get the flu I tell people I'm going to die, and they ridicule me.

> So just to prove these doubters wrong you'd be happy for flu to kill you?

> When you put it like that, it sounds ridiculous. But yes. Yes I would.

> If nothing else, you are a very petty little man.

Contagion's tagline is 'nothing spreads like fear', but that's not really true. Viruses, arguably, spread faster. In the face of a pandemic, making people afraid enough to avoid all risk of catching the disease is half the battle. Unfortunately, viruses have evolved to win the battle. That's why they spread faster than fear.

Viruses are extraordinary things. We say 'things' because we don't know what they are, exactly. Biologists don't agree on whether they are alive – viruses sit right on the line between chemistry and biology, and they sit in a very menacing pose.

Perhaps the best way to think about viruses is as computer programs written in DNA, the molecule used to replicate biological machines (sometimes it's a related chemical, RNA). The program goes something like this:

1 Roam around until you find a molecular machine capable of replicating your DNA/RNA strand.
2 Take over that machine.
3 Replicate your DNA/RNA and create protein shields to protect it.
4 Assemble everything into a new virus particle.
5 Get out of there.
6 Go to point 1.

Viruses aren't evil, as such. They don't *mean* to do you harm. It's just that executing the steps of this program inevitably causes you harm because the molecular machine they are looking for exists inside your cells. It's the act of breaking into the cell, taking over the machine and getting out again that leaves a trail of devastation in its wake. We're not saying they're sorry about it, but it's also nothing personal: viruses are actually indifferent to you. You're not tasty (see Chapter 3) or a threat (see Chapter 4); you're just useful and expendable.

It's probably worth noting early on that we could also be

talking about bacteria when we talk about *Contagion*. After all, they are deadly too. The Black Death that swept through Europe in the Middle Ages was the work of bacteria, not viruses, and it was as devastating as any viral outbreak has ever been. But at least we have some defences against bacterial infection these days.

Those defences are known as antibiotics. While it's true that some of our antibiotics are useless against some of these organisms (and some of these organisms are resistant to all of our antibiotics, which is dreadful in its own special way), we have NO technological weapons that kill viruses. None. We have some antivirals which can inhibit their spread, and our immune system can fight them to an extent, but there is no silver bullet against a viral infection. That's why, when you have a cold, your doctor tells you to just rest and please stop asking for antibiotics. It's the best hope you have of deploying your body's natural defences to maximum effect.

Ironically, viruses do have defence mechanisms that work against us. The main one is stealth. That DNA they are ruthlessly working to replicate is contained within a protein 'capsid' shell that your immune system doesn't actually recognize as a foreign body. The first your body knows about its presence is when a lollipop-shaped crowbar on the capsid shell pries open a cell wall.

Take the influenza virus. You might have heard scientists talking about H1N1 or H5N2: the 'H' is the lollipop-shaped crowbar. The molecule is called haemo-agglutinin, and it can take lots of different forms, each of which is designated with a number. The 1918 'Spanish' flu, for instance, was H1. In 1968, we saw H3 create a flu epidemic in Hong Kong. Every flu pandemic of the twentieth century brought a new H into the world.

How bad can it be?

Near the beginning of *Contagion*, disease control leaders gather to discuss what might happen. A central concern for them is R^o. This is the measure of how many new people will become infected by one carrier of the infection. The calculation is based on observing what has happened already in the outbreak, and the result will be affected by factors such as the percentage of people who have been vaccinated or local living conditions. If R^o is 10, each case will produce 10 more. The ideal would be a R^o of less than 1, which means the disease will die out fairly quickly. The 1918 Spanish flu's R^o was somewhere between 1.4 and 2.8. The virus involved in the 2014 Ebola outbreak had a similar R^o. That's not the only statistic you should worry about, though. The H5N1 bird flu virus has a R^o of less than 1 because it can't be transmitted through the air, but it is also frighteningly lethal, killing 66 per cent of infected people, compared to the Spanish flu's paltry 10–20 per cent.

The 'N' stands for neuraminidase. This molecule evolved to get the newly made virus particles out of the cell where they were assembled; it's a kind of glass cutter that slices through a cell wall. This, too, comes in many variants. In all, we know of eighteen Hs and eleven Ns.

This variation is part of the problem with viruses. There are so many different Hs because the RNA in influenza is a very poor copier of itself. The result of this is tiny changes in its make-up. This unceasing evolution makes it difficult for our immune systems to recognize it as a threat. The H is the only trigger our immune systems recognize, but if it changes shape just enough, there's a good chance the immune system won't spot it. This is one reason why we have to make a new flu vaccine every year. It's also why the HIV virus has been so devastating. It copies its own RNA so roughly that it evolved ridiculously fast, and our immune systems simply can't learn what to look for.

So, perhaps we should see viruses as cool, deadly, dispassionate killers: the psychopaths of the microscopic world. It's worth noting, too, that there are viruses that infect fungi, bacteria, insects and plants. They are part of the rich tapestry of life – and, astonishingly, you wouldn't be alive without them.

Somewhere up to 8 per cent of your genome – the instructions to make a copy of you – is composed of viral DNA. Roughly 100,000 pieces of your genetic make-up come from a particular kind of virus called a retrovirus, which inserts bits of its own genome into the DNA of cells it has infected. If it happened to infect sperm and egg cells, that viral DNA got passed on to the next generation.

In the past, our biology has occasionally put this DNA to work. Researchers now think that mechanisms as diverse as the immune system response and a placenta's protection of a growing foetus involve recruiting the facilities encoded in retroviral DNA that entered our ancestral genome more than 100 million years ago. So, although the virus feels like the bad guy in *Contagion*, know that viruses have already saved your life.

How Do Epidemics Begin?

> I've always liked the quote 'somewhere in the world, the wrong pig met up with the wrong bat', because it implies that somewhere else in the world, the right pig is meeting the right bat.

> Sounds more like the set-up for an animated romcom.

> Yes, which I'd happily watch. I find all these films about death quite depressing.

> Well I suppose you are statistically, and medically, much closer to death than me.

In *Contagion*, we learn (spoiler alert) that the devastating, world-changing, havoc-wreaking virus was brought into the world after a bat dropped a piece of banana into a pig pen. If there's one thing worse than a virus existing inside an animal, it's a virus that starts in one species and ends up in another.

Many viruses exist inside certain species without causing any harm. The bats that sparked the 2014 Ebola epidemic in West Africa, for instance, were 'reservoirs': they had the virus in their system but for reasons that are still debated, it triggered no symptoms. The problem arose when humans came into contact with the bats, giving the virus a new world of cellular machineries to explore.

As far as scientists can guess from tracing the roots of the 2014 Ebola epidemic, the whole thing may well have started with a toddler called Emile Ouamouno. In December 2013, Emile was playing in the roots of a bat-infested tree in Meliandou, a village in the south-east of Guinea. According to the villagers, he was grabbing and poking the bats. Toddlers being toddlers, it's very likely he came into contact with bat droppings, with some ending up on his fingers, under his fingernails and, eventually, in his mouth. Whatever the exact route, the virus got into Emile's body and he died a short while later. Within weeks, Ebola was rampaging across West Africa.

We first learned such cross-species transmission was possible back in 1933. A British researcher was working with ferrets that had been deliberately infected with influenza. One sneezed in his face, and he became ill. The scientists then worked out that they could transmit their own virus back to the ferrets. Presumably with some retaliatory sneezing.

This animal to human story is now familiar to virus researchers. In fact, in this century, three-quarters of new infectious diseases affecting humans have come from animals. Take HIV, for example. From genetic analysis, it seems that HIV arose from simian immunodeficiency virus (SIV) found in West African chimpanzees. Widely hunted for meat in the region, someone came into contact with infected blood and provided an environment in which the virus could mutate into the human form.

Mutation is key to the virulence of a virus. Essentially, different strains of the same virus can swap genetic material in a weird kind of viral sex. Often the new acquisitions don't make much difference, but occasionally they are game-changers. In influenza, for instance, the result can be a new H or a new N. And that can mean a flu virus that has never infected humans suddenly possesses exactly the H it needs to bind to the receptors on human cells.

If the environmental conditions provide lots of opportunities for viral sex with multiple partners, the chances of something new and dangerous arising are heightened. That's why many experts on viruses warn that modern ways of life are facilitating viral orgies. Take factory farming, for example. In China, California and the American Midwest, agricultural operations known as 'concentrated animal feeding operations' (CAFOs) bring together cows, pigs, geese, turkeys, chickens and anything else that can turn feedstock into a fat profit for the owners. These vast sites are awash with waste products and if the strictest food and hygiene regulations aren't adhered to impeccably – which you have to concede is possible – the virus-laden faeces of one species will get into the food or drinking water of another. Inside the stomach of the second species, the virus will find a host of cousins with whom it can swap genetic material.

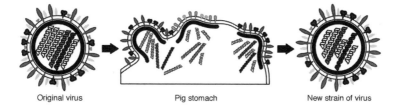

Original virus   Pig stomach   New strain of virus

In a suitable environment, a virus will gather and swap genetic material, emerging as a different strain

It wouldn't be the first time such a thing happened. The Spanish flu killed somewhere between fifty and 100 million people in the early part of the twentieth century. Scientists who have attempted to trace its origins report that the virus contains genes from domestic birds – chickens, for example

– and wild ones, such as ducks. There's also a genetic component from horses, donkeys and mules, which might have aided the jump to humans that were, at that time in history, constantly close to these animals.

Once we realized that the cells in the lining of a pig's respiratory tract, for instance, are coated with receptors that allow both bird and human flu to bind to them, we knew we might have a problem with insufficiently regulated CAFOs. Put pigs in the same space as birds and humans, and bird flu viruses have the perfect opportunity to become infectious to humans. The emergence of a significant pathogen from such cavalier operations seems to be a matter of when, not if.

Not that CAFOs are the only potential source of a *Contagion*-like outbreak. Anywhere people are living in close proximity with animals is potentially a big risk. We've already met one ill-fated toddler. Lam Hoi-Ka, a three-year-old from Hong Kong, is another. He died in May 1997 of H5N1 bird flu. We don't know how he caught it, but doctors quickly recognized the horrific symptoms (among other things, his blood curdled) and declared that anyone showing similar symptoms should be isolated immediately. Fortunately, H5N1 hasn't evolved a mechanism that allows it to spread easily between humans (a few genetic mutations might do it, but it's not straightforward even when scientists deliberately worked at making it happen). In the end, seventeen people were hospitalized, five of whom died from their H5N1 infection. The Hong Kong authorities killed every chicken on the island. But the disease still escaped – and it is deadly. Consider this: the Spanish flu killed just 2–3 per cent of those it infected. H5N1 appears to kill more than half the people it infects. And it is living in birds in at least sixteen countries.

That's hardly surprising when you stop and think about it.

In the twenty-first century, a virus can travel across the globe with unprecedented ease. Which is good news for the viruses, but very bad news for us.

Do Viruses Always Spread Like Wildfire?

What would you do if you caught the virus in *Contagion*?

I'd offer myself up as a vaccine guinea pig.

Oh, classic you. Sounds altruistic, but actually – isn't.

So what would you do, Mother Teresa?

I'd get my agent to pitch a first-person, follow-me-to-the-grave TV documentary. I'm more upfront about my narcissism.

Much of the suspense of *Contagion*'s story comes from the knowledge of a hidden threat just waiting to pounce. The lingering shots of the surfaces that infected people have just touched are surprisingly disturbing. And we should be disturbed. We should fear the fomites.

Every time you have a virus on your hand and it gets smeared on to an object – a doorknob or an elevator button – that object becomes a 'fomite'. The word comes from the

Latin word for 'tinder' because a sixteenth-century Italian doctor recognized that such contaminated surfaces could start the fire of contagion.

Fomites – objects or surfaces that host freestanding virus or bacterial particles – are everywhere in the modern world, especially where hordes of people are moving quickly through a space. In 2017, microbiologist Paul Matewele swabbed London's public transport system in eighty different places. He found that seats, rails, walls and doors were awash with bacteria. The tube lines were host to ninety-five different types of bacteria. Taxis had somewhere around forty and buses had thirty-seven. Some of these varieties were among the type labelled 'antibiotic-resistant'. There is, it seems, cause for concern. We can add to the advice in the film that Dr Erin Mears gives the hapless stooge on the bus. Yes, don't talk to anyone. Don't touch anyone. But also, don't touch any*thing*. You'll be creating deadly fomites.

Fomites play a significant part in the spread of certain contagions. The Ebola virus, for instance, isn't spread through sneezing or coughing. It's spread through touching contaminated bodies, faeces, vomit, corpses, floors, walls, buckets, clothing – anything where the liquefaction of the victim's body has caused the virus to ooze on to it.

Plenty of other viruses create fomites, too. When researchers examine the places humans hang out, they find influenza on the towels of day-care centres and family homes; coronavirus on phones, doorknobs, toilet handles and computer mice; norovirus on drinking cups, lampshades and bed covers of hospitals and cruise ships; rotavirus on the refrigerator handles in paediatric wards; hepatitis on the glazed tile surfaces of bars; and adenovirus on the drinking glasses of coffee shops.

Keep the toilet lid closed, people

It's a known problem on aeroplanes: those violent flushes create perfect conditions for throwing a spray of aerosolized waste into the tiny air volume of the aircraft toilet cubicles. But it's not just a problem with airborne toilets. The medical literature tells of one person infecting 329 others with SARS via some dodgy facilities. In March 2003, a fault with the plumbing in the Amoy Gardens residential complex in Hong Kong caused a backflow from the drainage system when the toilets were flushed. This turned some of the toilet water into an aerosol spray that contaminated the air. The problem was made worse by powerful fans that effectively sucked the aerosolized water – and the viruses it carried – out into the bathroom.

A hundred years ago, all this was only a problem if you were in the locale of an outbreak. But these days, thanks to our global transport network and highly mobile urban populations, the outbreak can come to you. And it will.

'We've created, in terms of spread, the most dangerous environment we've ever had in the history of mankind.' That's what Bill Gates told a reporter from *Vox* magazine in 2015. He wasn't guessing about that; he had been looking at computer models of how past diseases would spread now. A new disease with the virulence of the Spanish flu, for instance, would thrive today. Thanks to the extraordinary interconnectedness of the modern world, with its cheap, ubiquitous flights, dense urban populations, crowded commuter trains and office blocks boasting mile upon mile of interconnected air conditioning flues, these days the Spanish flu strain would kill millions of people in a matter of months. To be precise, thirty-three million people in 250 days, if Gates's computer model is to be believed.

The scenario is remarkably plausible, when you think it through from first infection – patient zero – to pandemic. Imagine patient zero gets put in contact with the virus by, say, shaking hands with a chef who's just been handling infected meat and didn't thoroughly wash his hands. Her hands are now coated with virus particles.

A study of people in public places found that they touched objects in their environment an average of 3.3 times an hour. They touched their own faces 3.6 times an hour. In private, the rate of touching the face is likely a lot higher. In *Contagion* it's suggested as 2000 or 3000 times a day, which feels like an exaggeration. Whatever: now you've read this, you'll become aware that you do it *a lot*.

Every touch to the face is an opportunity for the virus particles on patient zero's hands to get into her mouth. Being on the skin isn't enough; it's vital for most viruses to be ingested into the stomach or lodged in the mucous membrane of the airways. That's when the lollipop appendage can grab on to a cell and crowbar its way inside.

Although the virus is hard at work inside her body now, patient zero isn't showing any symptoms... yet. But she – like most healthy adults – will be able to infect people a full day before any symptoms develop. So she is already dangerous. She could still be infectious for a week after she starts feeling ill. What's worse, if she is asymptomatic – harbouring the virus but never actually getting ill – she won't adjust any of her behaviours, maximizing the chance of passing it on.

For now, then, she just continues with her day. And if that day involves international travel, a lot of people are in trouble.

She might kiss her lover goodbye, unwittingly making them the recipient of virus particles that are placed directly on the lips and into the mouth. Then she might ride the bus, slathering virus particles all over the handgrip and the seat back that she uses to steady herself as the bus lurches through the morning traffic. At the airport she'll leave viruses here and there, but it's on the plane that the devastation of twenty-first-century life really happens.

Every year, three billion of us travel on the world's airliners. A 747 might be carrying 500 people. Old planes have air quality systems that aren't up to much. If it's a new plane it'll have the latest HEPA (high-efficiency particulate air) filters that'll catch 98 per cent of viruses, but frankly if a passenger is infected with a virus and starts to cough or sneeze into the air around them, that's immaterial. Passengers seated within a metre or so have a significant chance of becoming infected. If the infected person is cabin crew, people all over the plane are at risk.

The truth is, we don't know much about the exact numbers involved. There have been relatively few studies, and they all encountered idiosyncrasies in the way different airlines and different planes process passengers, airflow and cabin cleaning routines. What we do know is that delayed flights where the air conditioning is turned off while the plane sits on the runway could be especially deadly.

In 1979, an airliner carrying fifty-four people was kept on the ground after an engine failure. The ventilation system was switched off during the three-hour delay. One of the passengers had flu; within three days, 72 per cent of the passengers were ill with the same strain of the virus.

Are you a super-spreader?

Ever heard of Typhoid Mary? Her proper name was Mary Mallon, and she was an Irish-American cook working in the New York City area at the beginning of the twentieth century. At some point she became infected with typhoid, but she showed no symptoms of the disease. That didn't stop her passing it on to the people she cooked for. Researchers believe she infected fifty-one people. Even though only three of those died, she was forced into quarantine. Mary was kept in isolation for three years, after which she was released and told to find work outside the kitchen, which had provided optimum conditions for her infection to be transmitted. Unable to earn a decent income, Mary changed her name and went back to professional cooking. She infected dozens more people with typhoid before she was arrested and confined to quarantine again for the rest of her life.

Mary would now be called a 'super-spreader' of disease. Disease researchers see many infectious outbreaks where a small group of people is responsible for a large portion of the spread. There are plenty of examples of super-spreaders. A 1989 outbreak of measles in Finland saw one person infect twenty-two others. During the 2002 outbreak of SARS in China, one man infected thirty-three others, and another man infected 138 people during a Hong Kong outbreak of the disease. Over fifty people contracted Ebola from just two individuals in the 1995 outbreak in the Democratic Republic of the Congo.

Super-spreaders are hard to spot, but they tend to have lots of close contact with people, and avoid seeking medical help until they are experiencing debilitating symptoms (if they're not just carriers and don't ever display symptoms). If you know someone like that, and there's an outbreak occurring in your community, keep your distance!

It's not just planes, of course. Buses, trains, departure lounges, subway systems and shopping malls all provide conditions conducive to the spread of infectious disease. Whether it is an airborne variant or transmitted through touch, the sheer volume of people travelling around the world every day makes this the perfect time to be a human-infecting virus.

More than four million people go through the barriers of the New York subway every day, for instance. Around five million use the London Underground. Over the forty-day period of Chinese New Year, people make more than 400 million train and plane journeys in China. Any one of these, especially if they've recently been in contact with the wrong animal, has the potential to be patient zero in a global pandemic.

What Do Viruses Do To Us?

This film is not a great advert for Minnesota, is it?

No, although it wasn't actually filmed there. Unlike *Fargo*, *Purple Rain* and, my favourite, *Grumpy Old Men*.

 I must confess I didn't expect *Grumpy Old Men* to get namechecked in this book.

Did you know that Walter Matthau was hospitalized with double pneumonia straight after filming it?

I didn't. But I do know that Minnesota's produced a lot of Hollywood talent: Judy Garland, Josh Hartnett, Stifler from the *American Pie* franchise…

… and the film student who wrote the screenplay for *Grumpy Old Men*.

All this time I'd assumed your specialist subject on *Mastermind* would be quantum physics. How wrong I was.

One of the most chilling lines in *Contagion* lies within a researcher's appraisal of what happened to Gwyneth Paltrow's character. Once infected with the virus, 'her body had no idea what to do with it'. Unfortunately, that's not Hollywood exaggeration. It's exactly what we see when new viruses arise. And bodies that don't know what to do throw everything they can at the novel threat, possibly destroying themselves in the process.

There's no easy way to tell you this. Sometimes, viruses actually make you kill yourself. Not deliberately. The problem is, they trigger the body's defence system so strongly that it goes on a rampage. Ultimately, it destroys everything in its path – including your healthy cells. That's why the Spanish flu was, paradoxically, so deadly to the young and fit. These people's immune systems were so robust that, when they went out to fight the flu virus, the immune response didn't stop until the people themselves were dead.

The first thing an infected cell does when faced with a foreign invader is secrete interferon. This is a substance that prevents new proteins from forming. In theory, it means the virus can't create copies of itself, even if it has control of the cellular machinery. In practice, a lot of viruses have evolved to fight back, cloaking the fact that they've taken over. With the 1918 flu virus, for instance, interferon was hardly deployed at all.

OK, so the virus has started to replicate itself. Now the body is aware it has a problem, and the immune system deploys its second line of defence: immune cells. These release a molecule called cytokine, which sounds the alarm and summons more blood, and thus more immune cells, to the site of infection. When they come across a damaged, infected cell, the immune cells kill and destroy it.

The Barry Marshall story

In *Contagion,* Jennifer Ehle's character gives herself a dose of the untested vaccine, then exposes herself to the virus. She's lucky – the vaccine works – but it was a brave move. She does it, she says, because of Barry Marshall, who drank a cupful of bacteria to prove that they caused stomach ulcers. Marshall became severely ill as a result, but the experiment allowed him to disprove the received wisdom of the time, which said that ulcers were caused by lifestyle issues such as stress, smoking and poor dietary choices. He won a Nobel Prize for his work – and, of course, a place in Hollywood history.

With the 1918 flu, that action became a problem. The virus had infected enough lung cells that the cytokine response produced the usual redness, swelling, heat and pain of inflammation that comes after infection – but turned up to dangerous levels. Basically, the attack of the immune cells on the infected cells resulted in people's lungs being liquefied. This overreaction is known in the trade as a cytokine storm.

What about the infections that don't make your body turn on itself? They can still be horrifyingly deadly, as we saw recently with Ebola. The Ebola virus's chief skill is in getting out of your body. The easiest way to do that is to seep out in a wash of liquid. That's why the virus has evolved the ability to trigger vomiting, diarrhoea and even to liquefy your organs. It blocks your blood-clotting mechanism, so every breakdown of tissue results in bleeding that never stops, and the mucous membranes such as the eyes and the inside of your mouth will ooze blood until you die or recover. Every infected person is producing streams of virus-laden seepage that is extraordinarily hard to avoid if you're in the vicinity. Hence the terrifying hazmat suits worn by medical personnel trying to deal with the outbreak in West Africa.

Though we are focusing on viruses, it's worth mentioning again that they're not the only microscopic killer around. Bacteria can be pretty deadly too – as the Black Death made clear. In medieval Europe, 60 per cent of the population succumbed to the horrific modus operandi of the *Yersinia pestis* bacterium that caused the Black Death (also known as the bubonic plague).

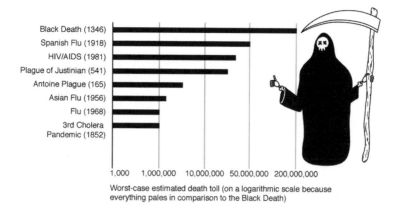

Black Death (1346)
Spanish Flu (1918)
HIV/AIDS (1981)
Plague of Justinian (541)
Antoine Plague (165)
Asian Flu (1956)
Flu (1968)
3rd Cholera Pandemic (1852)

1,000   1,000,000   10,000,000 50,000,000 200,000,000

Worst-case estimated death toll (on a logarithmic scale because everything pales in comparison to the Black Death)

History's biggest contagious killers

Once inside your body, the bacterium responds to the elevated temperature by altering the chemical structure of its external membrane. The alteration confuses the host's immune system, rendering it unable to recognize the bacterium as an enemy. Now it can swim its way to the lymph nodes where it replicates and proliferates to the point where your immune system can't help but notice something is horribly wrong.

And 'horribly' is right: eventually your blood is filled with bacteria swimming towards your lungs. The immune system's response is to overreact, destroying cells and, eventually, organs. If you are one of the unlucky ones and antibiotics don't help (or aren't available), you die from the effects of this 'septic shock'.

The Black Death is not just a historical disease. Every year in the United States, a handful of people become infected with the bubonic plague. They tend to live in the rural Midwest, where rodents such as prairie dogs and squirrels are commonly living alongside humans. These animals can carry the bacterium responsible for bubonic plague without showing any symptoms. When ticks bite the rodents and then jump on to a nearby human for a second blood meal, the unfortunate person can become infected with plague. Astonishingly, every few years, an American actually dies of the Black Death.

Anyway, back to viruses. Shall we just give rabies a tiny mention? This virus doesn't just take over your body; it also takes over your mind. Some viruses provoke actions – sneezing and coughing, for example – that help their spread. But rabies goes so much further. It stops you swallowing, for a start. The virus has to infect a new host through your saliva, so it doesn't want you putting the newly formed virus particles away in your stomach. What's more, it even makes you bite people so that you actively pass on the infection. It's astonishingly aggressive: when we sneeze, we might not be able to control it, but we (usually) do our best to make sure we don't sneeze in someone's face. Rabies stops us being polite – in, fact, it makes us the very opposite. Once infected, we become someone else, effectively: a zombie human, utterly controlled by the virus. It's frightening, yes. But on another level, it's also very impressive work from the virus.

How Do We Prevent A Pandemic?

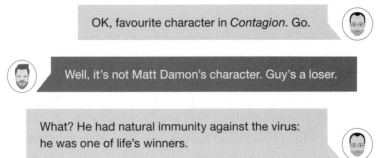

OK, favourite character in *Contagion*. Go.

Well, it's not Matt Damon's character. Guy's a loser.

What? He had natural immunity against the virus: he was one of life's winners.

Sure, but did you see what he was wearing? That anorak. My God, that anorak.

Really? Clothing choice is a measure of character for you?

You know what I always say – an anorak is worth a thousand words.

In *Contagion*, we see mass graves, shops stripped bare by looters and rioting on the streets. A real-life viral pandemic is likely to be no different. We'd better focus on finding a way out of this nightmare, hadn't we?

The first line of defence is isolation. Infectious diseases can't progress without a supply of new hosts. That's why one of the first countermeasures for an emerging epidemic is to isolate the infected. Put them in a room alone, or at least create a barrier between them and another potential host. Then the infection runs its course in the original host's body and ultimately fizzles out. Hopefully, the host emerges alive, but if not the virus or bacterium is at least condemned to death too. If they haven't got a living body to work with, flu viruses don't live for more than a day or so. Those that give you a cold can survive for a week outside the body. Bacteria such as the staphylococcus aureus bacteria that cause MRSA infections might still be viable after a few weeks, but isolation is definitely not in the contagious organism's game plan. That's why doctors concerned about the Spanish flu urged politicians to cancel rallies celebrating the end of the First World War.

Those urgings fell on deaf ears, unfortunately: on 12 October 1918, for instance, President Wilson led a gathering of 25,000 New Yorkers down the Avenue of the Allies. In the week that followed, 2100 New Yorkers died of the Spanish flu.

The Spanish flu, and other major episodes of global infection that occurred before the age of modern medicine, only ran out of steam when a supply of living hosts dried up. But the Spanish flu didn't kill everyone it infected. Those who survived were left with immunity – their bodies' natural defences would now recognize and fight off that flu strain as soon as it appeared on their turf.

Even more interesting are those with 'natural immunity'. In *Contagion*, Matt Damon's character is immune to the virus that's rampaging through the United States. That's not a convenient Hollywood sleight of hand; with every historical infection, there are always people who simply don't get ill because their immune system is, by chance, naturally able to recognize and fight off the infection. In fact, the virus wasn't fatal for most people in *Contagion*. Hollywood resisted the temptation to hype up the fear factor and settled for killing just a quarter of those infected, far fewer than would be killed by a H5N1 bird flu infection.

We can prepare ourselves in a way that significantly reduces the proportion of people that will be vulnerable to infection by a virus. The process is called vaccination and, if you and your parents have been sensible, it will already be part of your immune system's life story.

Vaccinations use disabled virus particles to train the immune system. The disabling means they don't have the power to make us ill, but the immune system doesn't know that. When they are injected into our body's tissue, the immune system takes a look at the particles, recognizes them as foreign and develops an 'antigen': a cell that can lock on to – and destroy – something with this particular shape. That means when the real thing comes along, the virus doesn't stand a chance.

See also

Hollywood has leaned on infectious disease more than once. *Outbreak* isn't as science-heavy as *Contagion*, but it's a solid tale of scientists working against the odds to beat an epidemic. Led by a perpetually worried Dustin Hoffman ('I don't want anybody working with me who isn't scared'), the team has to work against a military bigwig who wants the virus as a biological weapon. Watching this, you'll get a quick lesson in laboratory biosafety levels, and a good grasp of the perils of being a monkey in the vicinity of scientists intent on curing the disease you're carrying.

Scientists don't come off so well in *28 Days Later*. First, they create a virus that causes monkeys to become violent and aggressive. Then they don't implement security protocols that would prevent animal liberation activists from setting the monkeys free. The result is an epidemic (a local outbreak, in this case confined to the UK) of zombie humans displaying symptoms that suggest a combination of rabies and Ebola. It's not pretty.

Pandemic is very light on science, but it does open with a doozy of a quote, from Nobel Prize-winning biologist Joshua Lederberg: 'The single biggest threat to man's continued dominance on the planet is the virus.' After that, it's really just a zombie movie, with people moving through various stages of infection until they become 'Level 5', the classic mindless homicidal zombies.

Making vaccines isn't straightforward. As we've seen, viruses mutate, and last year's flu vaccine is probably unable to prepare your immune system for this year's strain of flu. That's why doctors' surgeries are issued with new flu vaccines every year. It's also why we don't yet have a vaccine against HIV.

But for some viruses, such as the ones that cause measles, mutation rates are low enough that we can be protected when we are very young. That's what makes the current measles outbreaks such a tragedy. There were more than 40,000 measles infections in Europe in 2018, and more deaths than we've seen in years. All preventable with a vaccine.

The MMR vaccine is astonishingly effective, protecting 99.7 per cent of people from a measles infection. Even more extraordinary is a new Ebola vaccine, which showed 100 per cent efficacy in trials. However, it is so far only effective against one strain of the disease. And it is impossible for us to prepare a vaccine against an influenza strain that is still evolving in the stomach of a pig somewhere in a shoddy CAFO in Kansas.

That said, we can at least prepare the facilities to manufacture vaccines when they are ready for use. In *Contagion*, the route to a vaccine rolling off the production line is a long, drawn-out process – and that's entirely realistic. First, someone has to identify the strain of the virus responsible, and check that it can be safely disabled and injected into a human body. But even when that's done, the level of the immune system's response has to be optimized. That's why vaccines contain various ingredients other than the disabled (or killed) virus. These are known as 'adjuvants' and they act as catalysts for the immune response. Only when the best recipe for these has been determined can we test the true efficacy of the vaccine. And only when that's been done can we start manufacture. Jonathan Quick, a notable expert on the pandemic threat, has worked out that it could take an entire year to get a new vaccine developed and distributed once a deadly virus has started to kill us off. The good news is, efforts are already under way to build a large-scale system that will dramatically cut the time between discovering a new killer virus and developing, testing and manufacturing a vaccine. That said, we haven't yet managed to replace the eighty-year-old trial-and-error flu vaccine programme that still grows its vaccines in chicken eggs. Quick recommends that we start to use newly available genetic technologies to develop vaccines that hit the unchanging 'handle' part of the virus's crowbar and could therefore work against both seasonal and potential pandemic flus. He also suggests that our medical researchers should step up global surveillance to help with early detection of a potential pandemic.

And you – what can you do? Stop touching your face.

2

Hollywood Wants to Kill You... WITH ASTEROIDS!

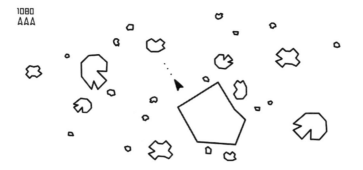

. . . .

'THE UNITED STATES GOVERNMENT JUST ASKED US TO

SAVE THE WORLD. ANYBODY WANT TO SAY "NO"?'

— *Armageddon* (1998)

. . . .

Armageddon is about a band of deep-sea drillers recruited by NASA to save humanity. A huge aster-oid is on a collision course with planet Earth and the

US military has decided that blowing it apart with a nuclear weapon is the only option. Unfortunately, strapping even 100 nuclear bombs to the asteroid's surface apparently won't cause enough damage. As one of the characters says, it would be like trying to stop a freight train with a BB gun. So someone has to drill down into the asteroid, drop the device into the hole and then trigger the detonator. And that person is – of course – Bruce Willis.

Do we need to add that it's not a true story? Probably not. But the science behind it is something that NASA has had to explore, because the premise is entirely realistic. A civilization-ending asteroid could emerge from the depths of space at any moment. What will we do about it? We're not yet sure, and *Armageddon* really does seem to provide some answers.

Where Do Asteroids Come From?

I'm sad that people think this is a terrible movie. Michael Bay said it's his worst. Billy Bob Thornton and Steve Buscemi both said they only did it for the money. Ben Affleck actually mocks it on the DVD commentary.

You know who else thinks it's terrible? NASA. They show it to all their trainee managers.

Why? So they can all be a bit more like Billy Bob Thornton?

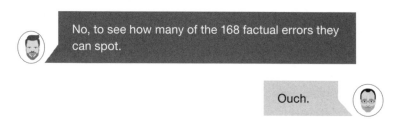

It might surprise you to learn that the central idea in *Armageddon*, summed up in the line, 'It's the size of Texas, Mr President!' is not entirely fiction. Earth is bombarded by more than 100 tonnes of space rock every day.

Not all asteroids are the size of Texas, of course. Most of them are considerably smaller, and some are just a few feet in diameter. They all have one thing in common, however: they are the detritus of the solar system's formation.

Scientists don't all agree on the precise history of the solar system, but the general consensus is that it started to take shape around 4.6 billion years ago. In the vicinity of our newborn sun, gravity and the solar wind caused swirling clouds of dust and gas to form into the spherical objects we now know as planets. Some of them, such as Jupiter and Saturn, are mostly made of gas, with a solid rocky core at their centre. Others, such as Earth and Venus, are solid on the outside and liquid at the centre. Like those chocolates your nan likes.

What's clear is that not everything formed such neat, round, satisfying objects. Some of the dust and rubble coalesced without creating a sphere. Other bits were thrown out from the collision of large space rocks that would form planets. The heat of such a collision didn't last, and the molten material solidified in lumpy shapes that wandered through the void until trapped in a circular or elliptical orbit. These ugly brutes are the asteroids.

And they are legion: our solar system contains billions of asteroids. For the most part, they live in the 'asteroid belt', an otherwise empty space between the orbits of Mars and Jupiter. However, they occasionally get diverted by a gravitational tug. That's when they come out of the asteroid belt and hurtle through the solar system, raining havoc on anything in their way.

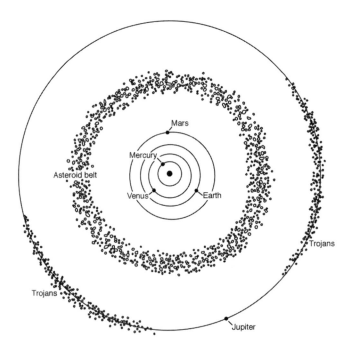

Most asteroids hail from just two orbits in our solar system

To see the effects of this, look up at the moon next time it's visible. All those craters you can see – there are thousands of them – are caused by impacts with rampaging solar system debris. The largest of them are over 1000 kilometres in diameter, so the pitted surface of the moon provides a very good reason to think about asteroid impacts with Earth.

Perhaps this is a good time to admit that we might have slightly misled you. Yes, Earth is hit by 100 tonnes of space rock every day, but not all of that actually hits the planet's surface. Only rocks bigger than 100 metres in diameter survive the descent through the atmosphere – the rest just get burned up by friction. But that still leaves a lot of potentially dangerous material: we know there are rocks in our solar system that are hundreds of miles across. They are orbiting the sun, and tumbling around their own axes, feeling the gravitational pull of the rest of the solar system's inhabitants. If a shift in the gravitational pull ever jerks them out of orbit, they could well end up on a collision course with us.

How an asteroid escapes its confinement in the asteroid belt has been the subject of a lot of research. The trouble is, it's actually very difficult to say anything for sure. Back in Isaac Newton's time, scientists believed in the 'clockwork heavens', where everything was predictable. Now, though, we have an appreciation of chaos – and chaos changes everything.

Chaos theory is a bit like the children's nursery rhyme where a king loses his kingdom just because there wasn't a nail to shoe a horse. It's all about an outcome that changes radically if the starting conditions change just a tiny bit. In the heavens, that can be a tiny shift in a planet's orbit, or where the gravitational pull from two planets tugs an asteroid in exactly the same direction for a brief moment. That can be enough to pull the asteroid out of its established, balanced, cyclic orbit in the asteroid belt and send it hurtling into interplanetary space.

The crater good

We aren't grateful enough to the asteroids. Before the Chicxulub impactor hit Mexico's Yucatán Peninsula, our mammalian forebears spent their lives scrabbling around in the dark.

That's because the dinosaurs were active in the daytime. Being cold-blooded reptiles, they were unable to function well until the sun had warmed them through, but once they were toasty and livened up, their sharp eyesight, sharp claws and even sharper teeth were a danger to everything in sight. Which meant the creatures sharing the planet with them had to keep their heads down and evolve physical traits that work well in the dark.

Think about mammals for a moment. Many of them have whiskers, a well-developed sense of smell and acute night vision. In other words, they're equipped for the night shift. Many of them are more active at night than in the day, too. Is this all evidence that the dinosaurs ruled the day?

A 2017 study gives us a clue to the answer. The evidence from genetic analysis of 2415 living mammalian species traced the emergence of daytime activity. The researchers found that the dawn of the sun-loving mammal was about 200,000 years after the Chicxulub impact. In evolutionary terms, that's no time at all.

Even more interesting is the fact that the first mammals to emerge blinking into the light were the ancestors of modern primates. This may explain why we all have relatively good colour vision and a poorer sense of smell and hearing than most other mammals.

Gravity is not the only force acting on asteroids, though. In 1900, Polish engineer Ivan Yarkovsky worked out that if an asteroid floating through space is heated by the sun for a few hours it will re-emit that thermal radiation after the asteroid's 'day' is over and it is no longer being heated. Overall, that emitted radiation leaves the surface in a slightly different direction from the direction of the incoming radiation. Because radiation applies a tiny pressure to a surface (whether coming or going), that means the asteroid will feel a small push in a direction that depends on its orientation and spin. So anyone wanting to work out whether an asteroid might pose a danger also has to take this – known as the Yarkovsky effect – into account.

That's assuming they spot it in the first place.

Who's On Lookout Duty?

Who are you most like in Bruce Willis's team?

Ben Affleck, I'd say. Handsome, skilled, brave, a bit of a maverick. You?

I think you're more like Rockhound.

Because, although dour and a bit sleazy, he's always right?

Two out of three ain't bad.

Maybe you don't remember 11 March 1998. You should be glad. There were some scary things happening – Celine Dion's 'My Heart Will Go On' was at number one in the UK charts, for example – but none more scary than an announcement from astronomers that they had found an asteroid that was on a collision course with Earth.

The asteroid was called 1997 XF11 and it was half a mile wide. The impact, which was predicted for 2028, would be utterly devastating if the astronomers had the trajectory right. It made the newspapers across the globe, including the front page of the *New York Times*.

Don't panic: the 2028 impact is not actually going to happen. The announcement came from the Minor Planet Center in Cambridge, Massachusetts, but it was only meant to be a preliminary call to other astronomers to check their data. Further analysis found that 1997 XF11 would not come anywhere near our planet. (This is true as we go to press. If you're reading this in 2029, after an impact-induced apocalypse, we can only apologize for the confusion; asteroid trajectory mapping is an imprecise science.)

However, something good came of the furore surrounding the announcement: it caused a sea change in thinking about asteroid warnings. In the summer of 1998, NASA founded a project called the Near-Earth Object Observations Program.

The initial aim was simple. Find, within a decade, at least 90 per cent of the thousands of asteroids and comets that cross Earth's orbit. Special attention was to be paid to rocks more than a kilometre in diameter. The aim has since changed a bit: NASA is currently charged with finding 90 per cent of objects greater than 140 metres across by 2020. The project has a new name, too: it's now the Center for Near-Earth Object Studies (CNEOS) and operates in conjunction with NASA's Planetary Defense Coordination Office (PDCO).

The details don't really matter, because we're already aware that the project is not going to meet its goal. That's partly because the budget hasn't been huge – as in the movie. In *Armageddon*, the President asks why a space rock the size of Texas wasn't spotted earlier. Truman tells the President the 'object collision budget' is around $1 million per year, which only allows them to track about 3 per cent of the sky. By 2002, NASA's equivalent had $4 million per year. The budget is now up to $150 million, but they still won't hit their target (ironically). NASA says it will only have mapped just over a third of the relevant asteroids by 2020.

After more than twenty years, we are aware of around 18,000 potentially dangerous asteroids. That's mostly thanks to a network of telescopes around the world. Astronomers use them to look for points of light that move over days, weeks, years or more. These are the asteroids and comets, and they crop up at a rate of about forty per week.

Once you've spotted these rocks, the next task is to check their size and trajectory. You'll be glad to know that the PDCO has a system in place for this. It's called Scout, and it computes the range of possible trajectories for newly discovered asteroids. If the results of those computations set off any alarm bells, NASA recruits astronomers to do more observations and pin things down as tightly as possible.

The twist in the tale is, we have managed to lose a few of these space rocks. When the telescopes don't report their sightings fast enough, some have disappeared from view by the time we attempt a second look, never to be seen again – until it's maybe too late, of course. When around one in nine of those are bigger than 140 metres in diameter, and therefore classed as 'dangerous', this revelation is a little unnerving. Some of these lost asteroids are as large as a few kilometres across. They may not be the size of Texas, but they are not inconsequential either.

Asteroid mining

We might gain the expertise needed to place a nuclear bomb on an asteroid from missions designed to strip the rocks of their valuable minerals. Asteroids are rich in many in-demand metals, such as gold, platinum, titanium, cobalt and nickel. In order to mine them, we would need spacecraft capable of flying to them, landing on them and performing drilling operations – just like what Bruce Willis achieved.

It's likely that we'll do it with robots, though, not with people (however charismatic they might be). Proof of concept came in July 2005, when NASA's Deep Impact spacecraft successfully fired an impactor into comet Tempel 1, creating a crater 150 metres in diameter, and sucking up some of the rock debris for sampling. Since then, the European Space Agency's close encounter with comet 67P/Churyumov–Gerasimenko via the Philae lander has given us even more information about space rocks. And we're even bringing home asteroid material now: NASA's OSIRIS-REx spacecraft had a rendezvous with the Bennu asteroid in December 2018 and dug out a sample that will get back to Earth in 2023. The Japanese Space Agency's Hayabusa 2 achieved a landing on the asteroid Ryugu, and is carrying out a survey of the rock before it returns a sample of the asteroid to Earth in 2020.

What's more, some astronomers estimate that we might not even have seen 99 per cent of the bigger asteroids. So it's tempting to conclude that, currently, the government-funded efforts are just not up to the job. That's why various groups of astronomers and space enthusiasts have lobbied for us to do more.

They are a stellar bunch (pun intended) including Kip Thorne, the late Stephen Hawking, Lord Martin Rees, Jim Lovell, Commander Chris Hadfield and more than 100 other scientists, artists, astronauts and performers. This group of luminaries (pun intended) has convinced the United Nations to declare 30 June 'Asteroid Day'. Their manifesto is that humanity can and must do better, and their tagline is excellent: 'The dinosaurs never saw that asteroid coming. What's our excuse?'

It's not just for fun: it's part of a campaign for more resources to be made available for asteroid-hunting. According to the Asteroid Day declaration, more than a million asteroids in our solar system have the potential to destroy a city. We have discovered only 1 per cent of them, and so must rapidly accelerate the programme to find and track these threats. They want to be detecting 100,000 asteroids per year by 2025.

Are they going to get their way? It doesn't look like it. NASA's decision makers decided not to endorse the two telescopes proposed for Earth's guard duty. The Near-Earth Object Camera, or NEOCam, was designed to sit in space and look for rocks with a diameter bigger than 140 metres. Even though a December 2016 report published by the White House's National Science and Technology Council said we've only found 28 per cent of the near-Earth objects (NEOs) of this size or bigger, the NEOCam programme has failed to secure any funding.

Our only hope is the Large Synoptic Survey Telescope, which is being built in Chile. Though it won't be operational until 2021 (fingers crossed until then), it will eventually be able to join the asteroid hunt. It won't spot the ones that are coming at us from anywhere near the sun, though, because it will be blinded by sunlight. It also won't see those that aren't terribly reflective. If it's a dark asteroid, it'll be a very dark day for all of us.

The story isn't over, however. An organization called the B612 Foundation, staffed by many of the people behind Asteroid Day, continues to push for governments to take the threat more seriously. It is seeing some success. In June 2018, for example, the US government recommended that we start to create designs for missions that will test asteroid deflection technologies. We may yet not require a team of drillers to save Earth. Or Bruce Willis.

What Would Be The Damage?

> Ready for some pleasing circular connections? That Aerosmith song written for *Armageddon* – 'I Don't Want to Miss a Thing' – was written by Diane Warren and nominated for Best Original Song at the Oscars.

> Is it written from the asteroid's point of view?

> What? No. My point is, Diane Warren also received nominations for songs she wrote for the *Con Air* and *Pearl Harbor* soundtracks.

Oh, I get it: they starred Steve Buscemi and Ben Affleck respectively.

Exactly. Even better, the video for the *Pearl Harbor* song was directed by Michael Bay.

Wow. It's the circle of life, isn't it?

No, that was in *The Lion King*.

Armageddon is a warning to us all. In his narration, Charlton Heston tells us, 'It happened before, it will happen again, it's just a question of when.' And he's right. Experts looking at the abundance and trajectories of rocks roaming through the solar system, as well as impact craters on Earth and the moon, reckon that Earth will experience an asteroid impact equivalent to 10,000 megatonnes of TNT every 100,000 years. That would destroy a whole country. The frequency of a global impact like the Chicxulub rock that killed off the dinosaurs should be 1 every 500,000 years. But since Chicxulub was sixty-six million years ago, our own Armageddon is kind of overdue.

That's one of the reasons why, in January 2016, experts came together in the Detecting and Mitigating the Impact of Earth-Bound Near-Earth Objects (DAMIEN) working group. The name was not an accident; someone involved had clearly seen the world-destroying intentions of *The Omen* films' anti-hero.

When the DAMIEN group published its report in 2018, it tried to strike a reassuring tone. There was, however, a hint of threat. 'NASA is confident that it has discovered and cataloged all near-Earth asteroids large enough to cause significant global damage and determined that they are not on collision courses with Earth,' it said. And then there was a 'but'. 'There is still some chance that large comets from the outer solar system could appear and impact the Earth with warning times as short as a few months.'

That would be a sobering moment. One warning in *Armageddon* is that, if the rock hits, 'Half the population will be incinerated in the heat blast; the rest will freeze in nuclear winter' (more about that in Chapter 10). But it's not just about us. As Billy Bob Thornton's NASA chief remarks, the incoming asteroid is what's known as a 'global killer'. 'It doesn't matter where it hits,' he says. 'Nothing will survive, not even bacteria.'

The chances are, though, we won't be hit by a global killer. After all, not even the rock that did for the dinosaurs sixty-six million years ago wiped out *all* life on Earth. Here, the culprit was a rock 10–15 kilometres across that created a crater 150 kilometres wide. It landed near the Gulf of Mexico, where it caused a massive tidal wave, or tsunami. The disturbance to Earth's crust created seismic events – which would have had their own tsunamis – as far away as Argentina. But it was the debris thrown up by the asteroid that turned it into a truly global event.

Deep beneath the surface of the Earth, there is a layer of rocks with a strange characteristic. It is a global phenomenon, found everywhere geologists look. These 'spherules' are what remain of the fragments of molten rock that were hurled up into the atmosphere by the Chicxulub impactor. Once they

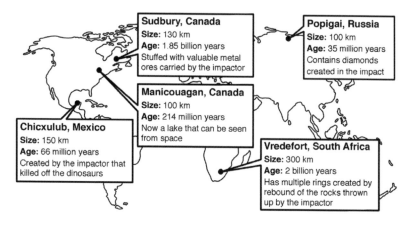

Sudbury, Canada
Size: 130 km
Age: 1.85 billion years
Stuffed with valuable metal ores carried by the impactor

Popigai, Russia
Size: 100 km
Age: 35 million years
Contains diamonds created in the impact

Manicouagan, Canada
Size: 100 km
Age: 214 million years
Now a lake that can be seen from space

Chicxulub, Mexico
Size: 150 km
Age: 66 million years
Created by the impactor that killed off the dinosaurs

Vredefort, South Africa
Size: 300 km
Age: 2 billion years
Has multiple rings created by rebound of the rocks thrown up by the impactor

Earth's biggest asteroid impacts

were 40 miles up – about forty minutes after the initial impact – they cooled slightly, and formed into round pebbles. But they were still hot, and the friction of the fall through the atmosphere made them hotter still. By the time they reached Earth's surface they were heating the air to an unbearable temperature. When they hit the ground, they were still so hot that they ignited searing wildfires.

Not everything that went up came down again so quickly, however. Another geological phenomenon, a global layer of soot, tells us that within a few hours a blanket of dust shrouded Earth. It stayed there for over a year, blocking out the sun and plunging the planet into a global winter.

The first day was bad. The first year was, arguably, worse. Plants couldn't grow in the poor light, and herbivores starved to death, eventually depriving other species of the means to survive. The base of the marine food chain, plankton, was also starved of light and ocean species toppled over like dominoes. Three quarters of animal species were gone. Relatively few members of the species that did make it through the first year would have survived for long – populations were drastically reduced. It was an evolutionary reset on a global scale.

But it wasn't all bad. In fact, we owe our existence to the Chicxulub impactor. It set a chain of events in progress that culminated in mammals dominating the planet. Eventually, an almost hairless cousin of the apes rose to the top, developing technology that transformed Earth and made its position as the dominant species almost impregnable.

Almost. But there's no room for complacency, as a couple of recent and significant asteroid strikes make clear.

On Friday 15 February 2013, an asteroid made it through Earth's atmosphere and exploded in the air over Chelyabinsk in Russia. It was only 17 metres in diameter, but weighed approximately 12,000 tonnes. It was travelling at 40,000 miles per hour when it exploded, probably due to intense heating within the rock, with a force equivalent to 450 kilotonnes of TNT. The explosion's shock wave damaged buildings in the area and people suffered injuries from flying glass and debris.

Then there was the Tunguska event of 30 June 1908. Almost miraculously, when an asteroid exploded over Tunguska in eastern Siberia with a force equivalent to 1000 Hiroshima bombs, no one was even hurt. That's because the region is remote and unpopulated; eighty million trees were felled by the blast. If that asteroid had exploded over a city, it would have been a very different story. The take-home from Tunguska is that humans have been very, very lucky so far. For a doomsday scenario, we'll need a bigger asteroid than Tunguska or Chelyabinsk. But it doesn't have to involve something as big as the Chicxulub impactor. It just has to hit in the wrong place.

Urban areas count for 3 per cent of the surface of the Earth, and rising. With increased urbanization, and new cities being built all the time, the chances of an asteroid strike having significant impact are ever greater.

Really, it's just a numbers game. A 100-metre diameter asteroid would cause a 4-kilometre-wide fireball, but people up to 40 kilometres away would experience severe skin burns. Buildings across the city would be levelled by the blast wave. If it hit New York, such an asteroid would kill approximately two-and-a-half million people.

If you want to kill ten million people, allow a 500-metre asteroid to hit Chicago. It would level buildings for 250 kilometres. If the same asteroid hit Tokyo, the death toll would be more like thirty million people.

It's not hard to imagine the consequences of an asteroid taking out Washington, Shanghai or London. There would be social, economic and political chaos. Even if the destruction is local, panic would be global because of the disruption to trade and communications. It's not ideal, is it? It's time to look at what we could do about it if, as DAMIEN says is possible, we might only find out it's coming with a few months' warning.

How Will We Save Ourselves?

OK, you've found out there are eighteen days before a global killer hits Earth. Are you telling anyone?

I'd tell my wife, obviously.

Why? What's to be gained by that?

I'd want to make sure we're together for our final moments. Are you saying you wouldn't tell your wife if the world was about to end?

No, I wouldn't. I don't think she'd want to know. It would only upset her.

You've used that line before, haven't you?

Here we go: this is the fun bit. In *Armageddon*, Bruce Willis and his band of brothers can save humanity with their drilling skills. In real life, that scenario is unlikely. But, like the asteroid, it's not a million miles off, either.

NASA engineers have come up with a number of different options for deflecting a killer asteroid. Let's approach them systematically, from the silliest to the least silly (none of them feel like a sensible option, unfortunately).

First up, we could paint it. Yes, you heard right. The idea is to paint one side of the asteroid in bright white emulsion so that it reflects sunlight better. That reflection is actually the emission of photons. The idea is that each photon emission will cause a tiny recoil, because every action has an equal and opposite reaction, adding up to a large force, and the asteroid will be deflected from its original course.

It's a theorist's solution, to be honest. After all, what are the practicalities of sending a team of painters and decorators, fully equipped with rollers and emulsion, up into space, then landing them on a huge rock that's hurtling towards Earth and – presumably – getting them off again when the work is done? Of course, if you really had to do it, you would probably do it with robot painters. But it still feels ridiculously impractical. And what if the asteroid tumbles over, meaning reflections from the painted side send the asteroid back towards us?

Moving on, then – and things are getting a little more urgent now that we've asked the painters and decorators to stand down – the next option is wrapping the asteroid in a shiny silver foil blanket. This essentially achieves the same thing as painting it, but with an added feeling of just-finished-the-marathon.

Alternatively, we could send up a fleet of mini robot space probes that carry concave mirrors. They would arrange themselves so the mirrors focus sunlight on certain points on the asteroid's surface. These points would get so hot that the rock vaporizes, ejecting material and creating a force that pushes the asteroid off its collision course. We don't really have that capability yet, though, and we're unlikely to start developing fleets of robotic space probes just in case. But the clock is ticking...

Technologists are not done yet. Maybe we don't need a fleet of space probes, they suggest; maybe we just need one really good one that's capable of shooting an ion beam at the asteroid. A beam of charged particles would knock into the asteroid and push it off course. The problem is, achieving a big enough diversion might take a couple of years – and we may not have that amount of time. The same is true for the 'gravity tractor', a high-mass spacecraft whose own gravity pulls the asteroid off course. It's too little – and probably too late.

It's time to get a little less subtle. We could fly a spacecraft into the surface as a 'kinetic impactor'. Maybe that would transfer enough lateral momentum to the asteroid for it to be deflected off its terrifying trajectory? We're going to find out in 2021, when NASA's Double Asteroid Redirection Test (DART) mission is scheduled to launch. Once in space, it will rendezvous at the asteroid Didymos, and eventually smash into its 150-kilometre diameter moonlet. A range of sophisticated instruments on board, and observations from Earth-based telescopes, will tell us how much influence the impact had on the moonlet's trajectory. Hopefully, it won't divert a huge chunk of the asteroid our way.

OK, enough with the guided missiles; what about a good old-fashioned *Armageddon*-style bomb? Amazingly, that's actually the preferred option of an artificial intelligence (AI) commissioned to evaluate all possible options. In 2018, researchers at NASA's Frontier Development Lab invented the Deflector Selector, a machine learning algorithm that looks at asteroid threats and decides the best course of action. This AI says the *Armageddon* scenario is officially the best. Hollywood for the win!

So, how do we do it? Well, ideally, we'll need to know how solid the asteroid is. If it isn't solid enough, the shock wave will be absorbed within the rock and not do sufficient damage. Or it might break up too easily, leaving us to deal with the 'shotgun effect', where one asteroid turns into many smaller but still dangerous fragments.

Of course, it's unclear whether we'll have time for this kind of pre-mission surveying. Survey or no survey, one thing is clear: we're going to have to put the bomb inside the asteroid. Attach it to the surface and it's just another kind of push; what we need is a world-saving explosion that destroys the rock from the inside. We still don't need to get Bruce Willis on the phone, however, because we could build a spacecraft that will do the job without his help.

Nukes in space

It's all very well for NASA to give Bruce Willis and his crew a nuke to take into space, but how would the Americans have felt if other spacefaring regimes – China, or Russia, say – had done the same?

The closest we've ever got to a space nuke is Starfish Prime. This was a 1.4-megaton nuclear bomb that the United States detonated 400 kilometres above Earth's surface, 1500 kilometres west-south-west of Hawaii. The July 1962 detonation, which was part of the US weapons testing programme during the Cold War, created a much larger electromagnetic pulse than expected, disrupting communications and damaging electronics in Hawaii.

Putting weapons all the way up in space is a very thorny issue in twenty-first-century diplomacy. The 1967 Outer Space Treaty, which has been signed and ratified by 109 countries, including the US, Russia and China, forbids any nation from placing weapons of mass destruction in Earth's orbit. Neither can they be put on the moon or stationed in outer space in any other way. No big weapons tests are allowed, either, which means practising the nuclear-powered destruction of an asteroid is probably not acceptable. If and when we do it, we'll do it for real.

The problem is, the Outer Space Treaty doesn't specifically outlaw the use of smaller-scale weapons, such as satellite-destroying laser beams, communications-jamming technology and even missile defence systems (see Chapter 6 for more on this). These are all beginning to be built, tested and deployed. A new treaty, 'The Prevention of an Arms Race in Outer Space'

(PAROS) is on the table, but so far it isn't proving terribly appealing to anyone. We may not have nukes up there, but space is no longer a weapon-free zone.

An option already on the table is the Hypervelocity Asteroid Intercept Vehicle, or HAIV. This is a spacecraft designed by Bong Wie, a State University of Iowa engineer. Wie and his collaborators have realized that the best scenario is to get up to the asteroid as quickly as possible – hence the hypervelocity part of the name. However, they have also worked out that sending the bomb in at the spacecraft's normal flight speed would crush the detonator mechanism without triggering it. That outcome would see the asteroid carrying on as before. The world will still be obliterated, and you'll be nobody's hero.

The HAIV has solved this problem by having the vehicle split in two. The first part crashes into the asteroid's surface and makes a hole. The second part, which hangs around until the hole is made, is the nuclear missile that does the real dirty work. HAIV's designers reckon they can save the world from a 140-metre asteroid given just three weeks' warning. It's a little bit longer than *Armageddon*'s eighteen days, but it's not bad.

Then there's HAMMER, the Hypervelocity Asteroid Mitigation Mission for Emergency Response. Its designers have a better feel for acronyms, but are slightly more coy about their brainchild's capabilities. But they are also slightly more connected: HAMMER is a joint project of the National Nuclear Security Administration, NASA and the US government's Lawrence Livermore and Los Alamos National Laboratories.

HAMMER has an objective in mind: the 500-metre diameter asteroid Bennu. At the moment, this has a 1 in 2700 chance of hitting Earth on September 25 2135. Plan A for the spacecraft, which is 9 metres tall, is to give Bennu a nudge, flying into the asteroid and pushing it off course. Given a decade of lead time to work with, a single HAMMER rocket could deflect a 90-metre diameter asteroid enough for it to miss Earth. As Bennu is bigger, we just use more HAMMERs – maybe as many as fifty – each launched on a heavy lifting rocket.

If that still isn't enough, Plan B is for HAMMER to detonate a nuclear device above the surface of the asteroid. The forces unleashed by the explosion would vaporize the surface, causing a recoil that might be enough to save the world.

See also

Deep Impact features a comet rather than an asteroid, but it's pretty familiar territory from thereon in. The threat is discovered by an amateur astronomer, the heroes are seeking to plant a nuclear bomb beneath its surface and the mission can't succeed without heroic self-sacrifice. Interestingly, *Deep Impact* opts to have astronauts trained as drillers, something that Ben Affleck suggested to Michael Bay on the set of *Armageddon* as far more plausible. Bay reportedly told Affleck to 'shut up'.

There was a lot of beef between the makers of the two films. *Deep Impact* came out first, and that might have been its undoing. On *Deep Impact*'s release, the makers of *Armageddon* were immediately handed extra cash to make sure their special effects were better than those of its rival. In the end, *Armageddon* won the battle of the box office. It took $554 million, blowing apart *Deep Impact*'s $349 million.

It might not be, though, which is why there's also a plan C: *Armageddon*-style nuclear bombardment from within.

So, whichever way we proceed, *Armageddon* is still the go-to scenario when our backs are against the wall. How big would the bomb have to be? Russian scientists have done the necessary calculations, based on their analysis of samples of the Chelyabinsk meteorite. They reckon that a 3-mega-tonne nuclear bomb would be enough to destroy a 200-metre diameter asteroid. Which is good news, because we know it's possible to build and detonate a fifty-megaton bomb: the Russians did it in 1961.

We are ready, willing and able. Yes, it's extreme, but so is the threat. As a wise man (Bruce Willis) once said, 'if we don't get this job done, then everybody's gone'.

3

Hollywood Wants to Kill You... WITH PREDATORS!

. . . .

'YOU'RE GOING TO NEED A BIGGER BOAT.'

— *Jaws* (1975)

. . . .

There's no shortage of scary predator movies, of course. There's *Alien*, and *Predator*, and *Alien vs. Predator*. And *Cowboys & Aliens*. And *Lake Placid*, *Arachnophobia*, *Anaconda* and many more. But *Jaws* is the granddaddy of them all. In Steven Spielberg's iconic movie, a fearsome great white shark called Bruce* terrorizes the small island town of Amity, ripping holidaymakers limb from limb. The shark in question is an absolute monster, measuring 25 feet from nose to tip. It's a bit of an exaggeration, but it doesn't really matter exactly how big Hollywood made it, because the real-world versions of these predators are fearsome at any size. The strange thing is, without predators, you probably wouldn't be reading this book – or any book. Outwitting our predators made us clever. Weirdly, it also gave us the resources to enjoy a scary film. So, shall we dive in?

Have There Always Been Predators?

My favourite fact about any film is from *Jaws*.

Is it that everyone thinks Spielberg intentionally doesn't show the shark itself until well over an hour into the film to ratchet up the tension, when actually it was because the mechanical fish kept breaking?

No, although that is a good one. It's about the scene where Richard Dreyfuss goes down in the cage and you see the shark. That's not mechanical. That's a real shark.

How do they make it look so bloody big?

---

* It's never actually named in the film, but the mechanical sharks used for the production were named after Steven Spielberg's lawyer Bruce Raymer.

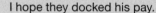

> They used a stunt double for Dreyfuss – a tiny one. Carl Rizzo was 4 foot 11 inches, didn't know how to dive and was terrified. And after the shark demolished the flimsy mini cage he was supposed to go down in, Rizzo refused to get back in the water.

> I hope they docked his pay.

Predators have a bad reputation. They are seen as vicious, single-minded murderers, often preying upon cuddly little animals that should be enjoying long cutesy lives. The grizzled fisherman Quint sums it up: 'Y'know, the thing about a shark, he's got lifeless eyes, black eyes, like a *doll's* eyes...'

To be fair, there's no getting around the fact that predators do kill. As Richard Dreyfuss's marine biologist has it, the shark is 'a perfect engine, an eating machine... a miracle of evolution'. For a predator, predating is in the job description. But that's OK, because predation has been a very important part of our evolutionary history.

Even before biological cells first appeared on Earth nearly three-and-a-half billion years ago, there was primitive life: RNA molecules floating around in a primordial soup. RNA molecules are both enzymes that catalyze chemical reactions and genes that contain instructions for making copies. That means they might have been able to self-replicate, meaning that natural selection would have been at work – if you're better at replicating, your lineage will be more successful, and more likely to survive. Some scientists believe that these molecules would not have been peacefully minding their own business – rather, some would have attacked others, breaking them down and effectively 'killing' them. In other words, behaving a lot like a predator.

One handy defence against such predation would be something like a protective coat. So it is certainly possible that the leap from floating molecules to simple cellular life within the shield of a cell membrane was an adaptive response to predation. Thank you, predator molecules.

And that's just the start of it.

There are two main forms of life: single-celled prokaryotes (very simple cells with free-floating DNA rather than a nucleus) and eukaryotes (more complex cells with a nucleus). All plants and animals are eukaryotic. The jump from a simple prokaryotic form to the more complex eukaryote occurred around two billion years ago and no one is entirely sure how. One theory is that a prokaryote predator may have gobbled up a bacterial prey (bacteria are also prokaryotic), which somehow survived digestion and lived on within the cell as what we now call mitochondria. Mitochondria, which have their own DNA, do the job of turning sugars, fats and proteins into the chemical energy that powers life.

One shortcoming of the theory is that it should still be happening, but existing prokaryotes don't appear to be doing much engulfing. However, we do see prokaryotic predators which are smaller than their prey – burrowing in and digesting from within. So maybe this is a better explanation of how a smaller cell might have ended up living inside a larger one, giving rise to a eukaryote.

While eukaryotic life is more complex than prokaryotic, to get to the diversity of life that we see now, another massive step needed to be taken – the leap to organisms that have multiple cells, aka multicellularity. And once again, predation may have played a role.

Researchers have shown in experiments that introducing a predatory microbe into the environment of single-celled eukaryotes causes the eukaryotes to evolve into multicellular forms within a mere twenty generations. That's quick work. It doesn't prove that this is what caused multicellularity, but it does prove that it's a candidate. What's more, we know that multicellular organisms can be bigger, with some cells performing specialized functions, and therefore better equipped to survive an attack. Apart from anything else, a multicellular organism can afford to lose a cell – a single-celled organism obviously can't.

Moving on to larger things, we know that the first animal life probably emerged over 600 million years ago, and not long after that (in geological terms, anyway) there was a huge array of creatures in our oceans. And in a hugely diverse and independent set of evolutionary processes, many of these developed skeletons and protective mineralized casings – much like the cell membranes protecting the floating molecules. By now, you won't be surprised to hear that many researchers believe this is also likely to have been a response to predation.

So what was the first predator that we would easily recognize as such? It's a challenging question to answer, since the fossil record is incomplete and soft parts don't tend to survive. But we can assemble a relatively coherent narrative from the disparate bits and pieces that we have found.

First, we can be fairly sure that there were no ocean-going large predators until 600 million years ago. A group of organisms called the *Ediacaran biota*, which ranged in size from millimetres to metres, were soft-bodied and mainly immobile, and should have presented an all-you-can-eat buffet for predators. And yet there is little evidence of predation upon them. So geologists assume the *Ediacara* were photosynthesizing for their food requirements, and there were no large predators around to disturb their idyllic lifestyle.

Escape to the land!

Why did fish first slither on to the land, about 370 million years ago, ultimately evolving into reptiles and amphibians? Because of predation. We don't know the details: they might have been chasing down the flesh of early sea-escapees like insects and snails, or they might just have been trying to evade sea-predators like sharks.

Amazingly, this – one of the great evolutionary steps – appears to be playing out again, right now, in the South Pacific. Blenny fish around the island of Rarotonga swim around in shallow rock pools at low tide but at high tide, rather than going out into the ocean, they wriggle up on to dry land. Researchers have calculated that this is because they are less at risk of predation up there, away from the predatory fish swimming in. This supports the idea that predation is a key driver in this process, and arguably more so than the hunt for new food supplies.

Some species of blenny have already made the transition to land. They still breathe through their gills by ensuring their gills remain wet, but they have also developed an ability to get some oxygen through their skin. They have also evolved stronger tail fins that allow them to jump around. We should give a special mention here to the epaulette shark, which also has the ability to wriggle around on rocks. Give it another twenty million years and we might have land sharks!

The first mega-predator we can solidly identify lived 540 million years ago. Its name is *Anomalocaris*, meaning 'strange shrimp' – and it certainly is strange. It's a freaky-looking customer, reminiscent of a crustacean, with big, powerful eyes and a large circular mouth surrounded by some grabbers, presumably to pull prey in. It could have grown up to 2 metres long: an absolute nightmare to fit on the barbie.

When palaeontologists first pieced *Anomalocaris* together, they thought it might be biting its prey. The mouth could close a bit and had jagged edges. However, that looks unlikely, because we now know it was simply too early in the story of life: it would be a while before proper teeth and jaws evolved. So they were probably just sucking up their food.

Anomalocaris weren't even the first large predators. Hard shells and exoskeletons had emerged long before they appeared, and in fossilized exoskeletons dating back 550 million years there are holes, believed to be bore marks where a hungry predator has been drilling through the tough exterior in order to access the tasty soft tissue beneath. The holes are all very similar in size and shape, suggesting that they were made by a single predatory species, although that species' identity remains a mystery.

Smaller predators have been around for some time. Amazingly, scientists have unearthed 740-million-year-old fossils of amoebae which have also developed tough skeletons. And some of these skeletons bear the marks of microscopic predation – tiny little bore holes, presumably made to access the nutrients within. We see this predatory behaviour today in so-called vampire amoeba. We can assume that micro-predation goes even further back – but with no hard parts to fossilize, we are extremely unlikely to find any direct evidence of it. Coming up towards the present, however, we do have good reason to believe that predation has continued to drive evolution: including our own unique abilities.

How Did Humans Out-compete Their Predators?

> Come on then. Ultimate top predator match up. Polar bear versus crocodile. Who wins?

> I'm not playing this game. It's ridiculous. How old are you?

> All right, how about tiger versus orca?

> It's not the choice of animals I object to, it's the whole premise. I'm never gonna derive enjoyment from pitting two magnificent beasts against each other.

> OK, fine, fine... anaconda versus eagle?

> Fair play, that's a good one. Stick me down for twenty on the eagle.

ook at us. Humans are – in relative terms – utterly puny. And seven million years ago, when the hominids split off the family tree from their chimp cousins, we were even smaller and weaker, with little brains and legs that hadn't adapted for running particularly fast. In other words, early humans made for perfect prey. When you look at the odds, it's a bit like when the marine biologist in *Jaws* laughs at the bumbling fishermen overloading their boat in a frenzied rush to catch the shark and says, 'They're all gonna die.' How the hell have we survived?

Well, it has been a challenge – a whole series of them, in fact. Any number of creatures have been out to get us, right from the start. And they still are. Writing from our safe haven in the south of England, it's easy to imagine that nothing is actively seeking out humans as food these days, but the global statistics tell a different story. Humans living near pristine natural habitats are being preyed upon by cougars in Canada, crocodiles in Australia, leopards and tigers in India... the list goes on.

The fossil record is shrill with the screams of human prey. Take the remains of the 'Taung Child', for example. This is a two-million-year-old skull of a young *Australopithecus* (the hominids that our genus, *Homo*, is believed to have evolved from). It has deep, raked markings which puzzled palaeontologists for many years. They have now been identified as evidence of a raptor kill. Raptors – more commonly known as birds of prey – have powerful talons, allowing them to hunt animals, including primates, much bigger than themselves. The marks on the fossil skull are identical to those made by modern eagles on the bones of their victims.

There's more grisly evidence of us-as-dinner. Another fossil hominid skull from one-and-a-half million years ago found in South Africa has two round holes punched into it. These holes match exactly the fangs of an ancient leopard, so it doesn't take a PhD to work out what happened. And there are some other very famous hominid remains, dating back to one-and-three-quarter million years ago, which bear similar puncture marks, this time matching the fangs of a sabre-toothed cat. In addition to huge raptors and big cats, we were likely preyed upon by hyenas, wolves, bears, snakes, and maybe even giant kangaroos. And that's why we evolved some pretty handy tricks.

If there's one thing more pressing than finding enough food for yourself to live on, it's avoiding being a meal for something else. You could call it the ultimate evolutionary pressure. For the prey, an interaction with a predator is a life-or-death situation. For a predator, the same interaction is just a meal gained or lost. Biologists Richard Dawkins and John Krebs described this as the 'life-dinner principle', and it drives evolution: if you can somehow evolve to be less of an easy meal, then pass that trait on to the next generation, that will help you and your species enormously.

Our evolutionary ancestors developed new ways to escape and avoid predators. We can see these adaptations in present-day humans. Our primal fight or flight mechanism, for example, is almost certainly a consequence of ancient threats from predators. The adrenaline shot that kicks in whenever we face trouble (or sometimes even the vague possibility of trouble) is the same hit that gave our forebears the ability to run quickly and instinctively from predators. Our hearts race, we hyperventilate, all in order to rush oxygen to our muscles. Interestingly, the after-effects of a fear-induced adrenaline rush are weirdly pleasurable, which is exactly why we like watching scary movies such as *Jaws*. There's also a vestigial hardwired fear of certain creatures that were once a danger, even if they no longer pose any threat; we're still nervously looking over our shoulders for a sabre-toothed beast. An amusing effect that lingers is goosebumps. Back when we had fur, the hairs standing up on end would have made us look bigger, a slightly less viable meal. Now it does nothing of the sort.

On the plus side, predators have made us sociable. Human social groups are pretty much universal. There are various theories to account for this, but a compellingly simple one is that there is safety in numbers. Having more individuals increases the chances of spotting the threat in the first place, and then if the threat advances anyway, a group offers more chance of repelling it with multiple teeth and hands. This is borne out in studies of existing primates: predation rates tend to be lower in larger groups.

There is even an argument that suggests we owe our ability to speak, in part, to predators. There are various ways in which primates try to avoid becoming lunch, including defensive attacks, freezing to avoid being seen, constant scanning of the surroundings and alarm vocalizations. These vocalizations serve a dual purpose – they alert the rest of your group to an imminent threat and they also let the hunter know that you have seen it. In the case of predators like big cats and snakes, for whom an element of surprise is crucial, they will slink off once spotted, and start again.

We know from extensive studies of vervet monkeys and macaques that many primates have different and distinct call signals according to different predator sightings, so one call might mean 'leopard', while another might mean 'snake'. And for each call, there seem to be corresponding actions. For the leopard sighting, get up into a tree, quick. For the snake, chuck stuff at it. These vocalizations are a key part of the primate defensive strategy and it's not unreasonable to suppose that early hominids were doing something similar. These calls may well have evolved to contain even more detailed information, especially if these hominids were living in open expanses where they would be able to spot multiple things of interest at once. The more sophisticated your communication, the easier it is to plan your escape. Language may have developed in part as a very useful tool for getting yourself out of harm's way.

The problem with language is, it requires a big brain. And brains are themselves extremely hungry, requiring a lot of energy to run. So for them to be worthwhile they need to be offering a lot of value to the animal. Studies had previously demonstrated a correlation between brain size and survival, but it wasn't until researchers did an experiment with big-brained guppies (well, bigger than an average guppy brain, anyway) and found that survival rates were increased, that we had confirmation of a direct relationship between brain size and survival. Yes, in guppies... but still.

One of the great conundrums in the evolutionary history of humans is how we were able to grow our bigger brains. We know when this started to happen – around two million years ago. This is about the same time that our teeth started to get smaller and our guts started to shrink. All of these things imply a change of diet. So how did we switch to more nutritious, easy-to-digest foods? How were we feeding those brains of ours? One idea is that we moved from scavenging and gathering whatever we could find, to more consistently eating meat. This would have been achieved by hunting. And here's the bit that's hard to reconcile – in order for us to eat and digest meat with our shrinking teeth and gut, we'd need to be cooking it. Heat effectively predigests food, allowing more calories to be taken in more quickly, which is great for maintaining and growing a brain.

The mastery of fire is absolutely pivotal for hominids. However, we can't find any evidence of our ancestors using and controlling fire until a million years later. Does this mean we just haven't found the evidence yet? That seems likely. As well as allowing us to cook, fire offers protection from predators: animals shy away from fire. And that may have allowed us to start sleeping on the ground rather than in trees – getting more and better sleep, which would have made us more vigilant defenders of our group and more successful hunters.

In fact, there is evidence to suggest that we were extremely good hunters – so good that we probably out-competed the Neanderthals and hunted many of the larger mammals to extinction. But, faced with the great white, we still can't claim to be the best.

Are Sharks The Ultimate Predators?

Did you know that Peter Benchley said he regretted writing the shark as a rampaging, cold-blooded killer?

Well, great whites aren't quite cold-blooded: they can raise their body temperature when they need to.

You're missing the point. He felt he'd endangered sharks by making people terrified of them.

People like Donald Trump?

> Exactly. Trump says he'll never give money to shark conservation charities. He wants them all to die.

> Well, that's good PR for sharks. Ever heard the phrase, 'my enemy's enemy is my friend'?

First of all, let's answer the obvious question: was the 25-foot-long shark in *Jaws* a realistic size? At first glance, no – and that goes double for the shark in *Jaws 2*, which was 30 feet long. And by *Jaws 3-D* (which you really shouldn't have watched in any number of dimensions) it was about 35 feet. The iconic shark from the original film poster was granted the most artistic license – the mouth is so big relative to the doomed swimmer above that some educated guesswork puts the shark at a whopping 50 feet long.

Your common or garden great white measures between 12 and 16 feet long. That said, they can be bigger: Peter Benchley's bestselling novel, on which the film is based, was inspired by the story of a 2000-kilogram, 17.5-foot-long great white harpooned off Long Island in 1964. The largest ever caught on camera is a female that scientists imaginatively named Deep Blue. She was believed to be around fifty years old, and an impressive 23 feet long. So maybe a 25-footer is just on the edge of plausibility.

Such a beast is the culmination of a multimillion-year story. In fact, sharks are one of evolution's most enduring successes. They branched off from bony fish over 400 million years ago, and since then they have thrived in every ocean environment on the planet. These remarkable creatures have lived through five mass extinctions, including the one that famously killed off all the reptilian dinosaurs sixty-six million years ago – and an even worse extinction event at the end of the Permian, 251 million years ago. This killed off more than 96 per cent of the planet's marine species and 70 per cent of its terrestrial life. But the sharks survived. In close to half a billion years, there have been about 3000 shark species. Nowadays there are about 500 species of shark, many of which date from the time of the dinosaurs. No wonder people sometimes refer to them as living fossils.

Almost everything we know about the evolutionary history of sharks comes from their teeth. The rest of the shark's skeleton is made of cartilage, not bone.* Cartilage decays rapidly in the sea so fossil remains are very rarely found. Fortunately, sharks have rows of little dagger teeth that regenerate, moving forward like a vicious conveyor belt to continuously replace the ones at the front which may be damaged or lost. A great white shark may grow between 20,000 and 40,000 razor-sharp, triangular, serrated teeth in its lifetime. So the fossil record is rife with them: good news for palaeontologists, and for people looking for a necklace to show they've been on a gap year.

That said, there are some records of shark skeletons. We've found a complete 380-million-year-old fossilized skeleton of one very early shark called *Cladoselache*, for instance. Its streamlined, torpedo-shaped body and forked tail makes it recognizably a shark – and one that would have been fast and agile through the water. The fossilized jaw shows it had strong muscles attached, giving *Cladoselache* a decent bite too: this was a top predator. In fact, sharks were some of the first

---

* This is what separates sharks from the bony fish – and of course us. Humans are ultimately descended from bony fish, which is why a salmon is more closely related to you than it is to a shark.

creatures to develop a jaw: a huge advantage that means you can start biting and eating things bigger than your mouth. Many scientists reckon the shark's jaw evolved from a gradual modification of the bony arches supporting the gills, and that this modification was probably being selected for because it improved respiration. But the fringe benefits – biting, gripping and generally terrorizing stuff – no doubt made this particular innovation into a keeper.

Sharks need your help

Many shark species are endangered because they are being hunted by a relatively new predator in the seas – humans. In 2013 it was estimated that humans kill 100 million sharks every year. *100 million.* They have been killed on an industrial scale for shark fin soup (the huge South East Asian market is predominantly serviced by EU-based fisheries), as well as getting caught up in other fishing operations. Once sharks are caught and the fin is hacked off, we have such disregard for these majestic animals that they are often just thrown back into the water to slowly die. The effect of wiping out shark populations is far-reaching because of their elevated position in the food chain. One group of sharks was removed from a reef near Hawaii because they were close to a fishery. This meant that octopus numbers in the area rocketed – because they were no longer being eaten by the sharks – and in turn crustacean numbers plummeted as the octopuses devoured them. Then eventually there wasn't enough food to sustain the octopuses, and their numbers also crashed. That's just one example of a catastrophic food chain disruption.

Cladoselache wasn't the only thing in the ocean with a jaw. Competition for food will have come from creatures like the catchily named *Dunkleosteus*. This armoured monster was the size of a bus and had the most powerful bite of any fish that has ever swum the Earth's oceans. It didn't have teeth, but sharpened bony plates that could have sheared through pretty much anything. Rivals like this may well have driven the diversification of sharks. The so-called 'Golden Age of Sharks' came 360 million years ago, in the Carboniferous period. This saw some very peculiar adaptations and body shapes, including a shark that had an anvil-shaped dorsal fin (purpose: unknown) and one with a spiral of teeth the size of a dinner plate protruding from its lower jaw (purpose: unknown). It must have been a hell of a time to go snorkelling.

Not everything managed to stay alive. For reasons that no one has managed to fathom, the unit we call *Dunkleosteus* disappears from the fossil record roughly 350 million years ago, for example. But no matter: every time a species goes extinct, a new niche opens up, and sharks have typically been expert exploiters of such niches.

This was particularly true with the mass extinction events – the recovery periods after these catastrophic times appear to be when sharks diversified the most. The one that ended the Triassic period 200 million years ago, for example, saw the development of a particularly useful feature: a kind of flexible, retractable jaw. This gives sharks a sleek profile when swimming, which reduces drag, and then offers a crucial little advantage when going in for the kill. As the shark lifts its head, the jaw rapidly protrudes out and grabs the victim, before just as rapidly tucking back in again.

The goblin shark shows just how useful a shark's
moveable jaw can be

But, impressive as they are, sharks haven't always had it their own way. Around the time they gained their flexible jaw, they lost face to evolving reptiles. Having spent some quality time on the land, the reptiles were now sliding back into the sea, and some of these new marine creatures were the most fearsome predators ever to roam the oceans. Even the sharks backed away from things like the plesiosaur, the pack-hunting ichthyosaur and the terrifying, 20-metre-long pliosaur with its 3-metre-long lower jaw. When we first started to find their fossils in the nineteenth century, they became popularly known as sea dragons. Nothing was hunting these monsters.

Luckily for the sharks, though, an enormous meteor hit Mexico (see Chapter 2), causing the mass extinction at the end of the Cretaceous period and killing off the marine reptiles. Once again, the sharks could rise to the top of the food chain. When mammals first started coming back to the water, sharks were ready. They'd grown big and agile, and were extremely interested in eating these blubbery, nutritious newcomers – seals and whales and so on. But sharks only remained the apex predator until killer whales swum into town. Even Jaws must bow to the orca: killer whales are far bigger and faster than a great white. They're also more discerning. While sharks will just munch through the whole of their prey, killer whales have been known to carefully extract the liver of a great white – a big, tasty, nutrient-rich treat – and leave the rest. However much you might fear the great white, you should double it for the orca. Maybe that's how Quint's boat got its name.

How Do I Avoid Being Lunch?

> This movie has an amazing legacy.

> Are you talking about the 2013 study that showed it still makes almost half of us think twice before getting in the water?

> That's good, but I was thinking about it being the first summer blockbuster. With *Jaws*, Hollywood hit on a new marketing model.

> And the idea of the blockbuster franchise, of course: money-grabbing, ever-poorer sequels.

> That's not always true. *Mama Mia! Here We Go Again* is no worse than the first one.

> Spielberg really did create a monster, didn't he?

Since we're focused on *Jaws*, let's start with sharks. There's an obvious strategy: STAY OUT OF THE WATER. But even that might not be necessary.

Jaws is predicated on the idea of a man-eater. Would a shark really develop a taste for human flesh? Sadly (not for Australians and Californians, perhaps), the evidence is scant. The average number of shark attacks on humans every year is around eighty, and the average number of annual fatalities is six. In 2018, there were just five. Which means that for every human killed by a shark, around 20 million sharks were killed by humans.

The truth is, great whites don't want to eat you. These sharks are picky eaters because they have very slow digestive tracts, and don't want to waste time and space in their gut by eating something as un-nutritious as you. However you might see yourself, to a great white you are scrawny and unappealing, especially when ranked against their blubbery, highly calorific food of choice: seals and sea lions.

That's why some people have suggested that human interactions were a simple case of mistaken identity. From below, a silhouetted surfer on a surfboard might pass for a seal; a panicking swimmer could be a floundering fish. But great whites have very good eyesight, and when these sharks have real prey in sight, they attack from below – bursting upwards at great speed to propel themselves into their victim. Observations of their style of approach to humans suggest something else is going on. They don't advance explosively, as they do with their prey. It's about as softly-softly as a giant killing machine can manage. They do a few circling passes and then come in for an exploratory bite.

So, the chances are, they're probably just curious. Not that that's any comfort when you've lost a leg. But it's not the shark's fault, exactly. It doesn't have an equivalent of a poke, or a handshake, or that thing your mum does when she's picking a melon in the greengrocers. If teeth were your only investigative option, you'd bite stuff too.

The best advice for dealing with sharks remains the simplest: if there's any risk, STAY OUT OF THE WATER. That's also good advice when it comes to crocodiles, by the way – although they can come up on to land, of course. If a crocodile or alligator slithers out of the water and starts charging at you – run in a straight line as fast as you can (the idea that you should run in a zigzag is a dangerous myth). The croc will run out of steam before you do and give up on its pursuit. If you're a bit too slow and it does catch you, give it a poke in the eyes. That might persuade it to loosen its grip. But, really, at that point you're dealing with an animal that has the strongest jaws – with the largest bite force – of any animal living today. So really you should have run faster. Don't say you weren't warned.

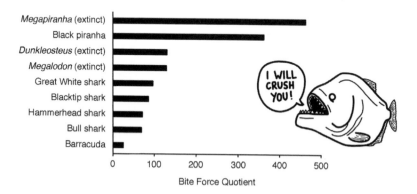

The bite-force quotient (the ratio of the bite force to the body mass) of some of the great aquatic predators

See also

In *The Meg*, rescue diver Jason Statham discovers a deeper bit of the Mariana Trench, and a couple of 75-foot-long prehistoric sharks – *Megalodons*. They get a bit overexcited and in the end leave Statham with no choice but to stab the biggest one with his submarine and then poke it in the eye with some poison. It is (wait for it) not based on a true story. However, these sharks certainly did exist, although it's hard to say just how big they would have got. We do know that they had huge, serrated 7-inch teeth, so assuming a body plan like the great white, they may have reached 60 feet. It was originally thought that great whites were direct descendants of *Megalodons*, but now we know that great whites are evolved from mako sharks. *Megalodons* first appeared twenty-three million years ago and went extinct about 3.6 million years ago. It's not entirely clear why, but probably due to increased competition for a decreasing food supply. Could they still be lurking in a hitherto unexplored part of the oceanic depths? Probably not. But maybe. After all, we discovered a new shark species as recently as 1976. This was an 18-foot monster that scientists called the megamouth shark because of its – oh, you can figure it out.

Whatever you do, do not confuse the advice for crocodiles – run like hell – with advice for avoiding animals like bears, big cats or wolves. Running from them is an extremely bad idea: it will make them immediately think of you as prey. That's bad news, because they will all outrun you over a short distance. Instead, try to make yourself look bigger than you are. Spread your coat out. Stand on tiptoes. Put your rucksack on your head. Anything. Just look big and the animal is less likely to fancy its chances. With big cats they tend to avoid attacking things that will put up a fight. With that in mind it might be helpful to throw stuff at a tiger – sticks, stones, anything. Try yelling as well. If you can just hold your nerve and stand strong, then it will think better of having a go. Hopefully.

Oh, and if you're still worried about a shark attack (which you shouldn't be: just STAY OUT OF THE WATER), there does seem to be one very effective repellent. It has been anecdotally reported since the Second World War that sharks avoid areas where dead sharks are decomposing. This makes sense: if another shark has been killed in the area, it implies that a predator or other danger is present. The good news is, a 2014 study confirmed that necromone, the chemical mixture given off by putrefying shark tissue, does indeed ward sharks away. So next time you go in the sea, just slather yourself in some responsibly-sourced old shark flesh and you'll be absolutely fine. Enjoy.

4

Hollywood Wants to Kill You... WITH ROBOTS!

'THEY SAY IT GOT SMART, A NEW ORDER OF INTELLIGENCE.

THEN IT SAW ALL PEOPLE AS A THREAT.'

— *The Terminator* (1984)

Whether it's murderous Stepford Wives, a callous Hal 9000, the ruthless Robocop or *Westworld*'s crazy AI The Gunslinger, who doesn't enjoy the carnage when a technology turns on its creator? But there's one bot that stands head and shoulders above the rest. Arnold Schwarzenegger as the Terminator is an icon, a byword for passionless, efficient execution. As Kyle Reese tells Sarah Connor, 'It can't be bargained with, it can't be reasoned with, it doesn't feel pity or remorse or fear, and it absolutely will not stop... ever, until you are dead.' Like all the best Hollywood villains, the Terminator is a product of our own fears. Put simply, the concern is this: are we already creating our own version of Skynet, the AI that deployed the Terminator in order to ensure it could subjugate the human race? Have we unwittingly sowed the seeds of our own destruction? Spoiler alert: it's a definite maybe.

Are We Any Good At Making Robots?

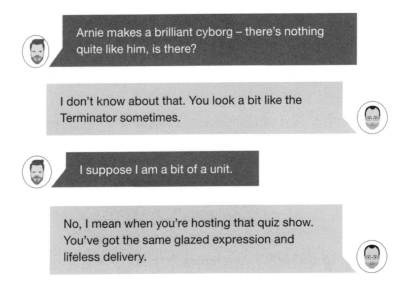

> **Arnie makes a brilliant cyborg – there's nothing quite like him, is there?**

> I don't know about that. You look a bit like the Terminator sometimes.

> **I suppose I am a bit of a unit.**

> No, I mean when you're hosting that quiz show. You've got the same glazed expression and lifeless delivery.

The T-800 Model 101 Terminator is a very well-made robot. Strictly speaking, it's a cybernetic android, or cyborg, because it is part-biology, part-machine. But it's still impressive.

And if we have any complaints about robots these days, it's that they just aren't very good. As Sarah Connor says in the fictional world of 1984, 'They cannot make things like that yet!'

For decades now, we've been watching sci-fi robots on screen that are far better than anything we have ever seen at work in real life. But that doesn't mean that the robots haven't arrived. According to statistics from the International Federation of Robotics, by 2020 there will be three million robots working in the world's factories. That's double the number there was in 2014. They aren't doing exciting jobs – that's kind of the point of deploying these robots, after all – but they are making a major contribution to economic growth.

It's not just in factories, either. Warehouses are starting to automate like never before. In the US, 2018 saw a 60 per cent growth in robots installed in food and consumer goods processing. In 2019, Amazon made headlines by starting to use robots rather than humans to package its customers' orders. And the construction industry, long thought to be immune to the robot revolution, is now seeing humans share sites with bricklaying robots like SAM (Semi-Automated Mason) that can build a wall faster than human brickies.

The mechanical advantage is that, if the work is repetitive, involves following straightforward instructions and requires a fixed set of programmable movements, a robot is probably going to do it as well as a human – and faster, with no toilet or lunch breaks, no risk of injury and no requirement for healthcare payments or days off. Robots will work the holiday weekend without complaining, and they never turn up for work hungover.

In certain sectors, robots have a different set of advantages. Take surgery, for example. We are already seeing robots perform intricate operations – but only as tools operated by surgeons. Sometimes that operation is from thousands of miles away; a surgeon can get a good view from the robot's cameras so doesn't need to be in the same room as the patient. Sometimes the surgeon's involvement is in the programming and supervision. There's no AI involved; robots aren't making surgical decisions yet. But they can make smaller, neater incisions than are possible by hand, minimizing the trauma to the patient and shortening recovery times.

Perhaps the greatest user of robots will be the sector that was the greatest innovator in the first Industrial Revolution. Farming has always been ripe for reinvention through technology. Food production used to be humans' sole occupation. Then the advent of tool use allowed it to become the work of a dedicated slice of the workforce while others focused on things like building or cooking. When agricultural machinery came along, many more people lost their jobs, but food production became cheaper and more efficient. Now the robots are entering the fields, doing jobs where humans are unavailable or 'uneconomic'. Robots that look for weeds and selectively uproot or spray them with weedkiller are far more cost-effective than a human weeder. Roaming machines that keep an eye on livestock in the vast expanses of the Australian outback are able to monitor cattle gait and body temperature, and report back on the state of the pastures that are being grazed. Australian farmers are grateful, saying they simply couldn't get human workers for these kinds of jobs. Farmers in the US are saying similar things: plant nurseries are using robots to move plants around their vast worksheds, space them out as they grow and prepare them for sale. It's not glamorous work, and buying in the robots has solved these firms' hiring problems.

Of course, these robots are hardly like those in the sci-fi visions of our future. We have been raised with the idea that robots will one day exist alongside us in our daily lives, as domestic help, bartenders and shop assistants. It's Isaac Asimov's automated leaders of society in *I, Robot* that caught our imagination, not the trash-sorting WALL-E.

One application is living up to our more glamorous hopes: space-faring robots. We humans have put robot explorers on the moon, on Mars and even on asteroids. It makes sense, too. There has been a lot of hand-wringing about humans not returning to the moon for fifty years, but it's hard to find worthwhile lunar-based tasks that humans could do better than robots – for now, at least. And as for going to Mars; it's still not clear when humans will be ready to do that (although Congress have set NASA the target of getting humans 'near or on the surface… in the 2030s'), while robots have roamed the surface of the red planet since 1997.

For sheer impressiveness, though, it's hard to beat the military-funded robots. Look at BigDog, for example. Created by Boston Dynamics under contract to the US military's Defense Advanced Research Projects Agency (DARPA), it's a packhorse of a robot: a massive beast that can handle pretty much any terrain with its four articulated legs, AI-fed brain and eerie ability to recover from being knocked around. If you haven't seen it, take a look at its YouTube videos. This is a robot that will make you feel just a little bit uncomfortable, because it actually seems to be closely mimicking what real biological creatures can do, and it's not small, feeble or obviously flawed. It weighs 109 kilograms, can carry a 45-kilogram payload and is powered by a go-kart engine that allows it to run at 10 kilometres per hour. It's a metre tall on four legs but when you're watching it, you feel like it could rear up on two legs, pick up a machine gun and do a pretty good impression of the Terminator.

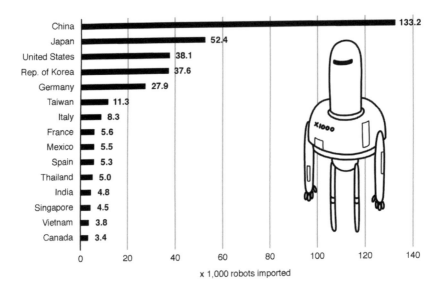

Country	x 1,000 robots imported
China	133.2
Japan	52.4
United States	38.1
Rep. of Korea	37.6
Germany	27.9
Taiwan	11.3
Italy	8.3
France	5.6
Mexico	5.5
Spain	5.3
Thailand	5.0
India	4.8
Singapore	4.5
Vietnam	3.8
Canada	3.4

x 1,000 robots imported

According to the International Federation of Robotics, China was by far the biggest importer of industrial robots in 2018

It won't, though, because it was designed to carry loads as a soldier's assistant – and because it's been scrapped. The official reason given for its abandonment was that its engine made it too loud for the battlefield; soldiers reckoned it would give away their position. BigDog's replacement, AlphaDog, has also been taken aside and (metaphorically) shot in the head – for pretty much the same reasons. Then along came Spot, a battery-powered reconnaissance robot the size of a large dog. But that was also unwanted in the end. It couldn't be made autonomous, so it had to have an operator, which kind of defeats the point.

The US Marine Corps Warfighting Lab (yes, that's a thing) says it's dropping the whole idea of giving soldiers robotic assistants for now. That's bad news for Boston Dynamics' Atlas robot, a humanoid that can do backflips, parkour and generally act like the annoying guy at a party who insists on showing off all his tricks. Though funded and overseen by DARPA (of course), Atlas is now being touted as nothing more exciting than a potential buddy for search and rescue teams.

Boston Dynamics is manufacturing at least one of its prototypes, though. It's a version of Spot called SpotMini. It has limited navigation capabilities – there's one camera for avoiding obstacles and a few more mounted around its body for looking out into its environment – but that's OK because it's designed to – wait for it – work in a factory. Sigh. At best, it might do a bit of patrolling round the factory grounds.

So, it seems that, apart from the odd robot vacuum cleaner, we can't get these things into our homes: it's still too hard. That's illustrated by what Boston Dynamics boss Marc Raibert told *Wired* magazine about SpotMini. It is well suited to working in multiple environments. But when he broke it down, it turns out that doesn't exactly make it all-terrain. Rather, it can handle 'street to curb, stairs, lips between rooms'. Lips between rooms: not terribly impressive, is it? Obviously, navigating the perilous territory where one room turns into another has challenged all of us at one time or another. But then we went to preschool (or sobered up), and there was no looking back.

However, just because legged robots are currently failing to stand their ground, don't think we're going to be spared the Terminator scenario.

Could We Create Skynet?

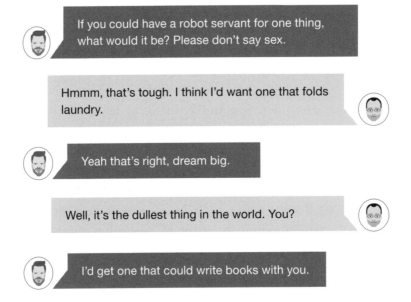

If you could have a robot servant for one thing, what would it be? Please don't say sex.

Hmmm, that's tough. I think I'd want one that folds laundry.

Yeah that's right, dream big.

Well, it's the dullest thing in the world. You?

I'd get one that could write books with you.

The system goes on-line August 4th, 1997. Human decisions are removed from strategic defense. Skynet begins to learn at a geometric rate. It becomes self-aware at 2:14 a.m. Eastern time, August 29th. In a panic, they try to pull the plug.

In the *Terminator* films, the US military developed an artificially intelligent data network called Skynet. They used it to control their array of sophisticated defence technologies, including the US nuclear arsenal. When Skynet suddenly developed self-awareness, panicking operators tried to shut it down, an action the network saw as an attack. It initiated a nuclear strike against Russia, the Russians retaliated, billions of people died and the post-apocalyptic world was not a terribly happy one.

In our world, 29 August 1997 was actually the day that Netflix was launched. We're pretty sure that its algorithm isn't self-aware, but is it possible for a computer, or a network of computers, to wake up? Could we ever enter a scenario where an AI begins to put its own interests – or at least its own sense of purpose – first?

This is a tough one. We've come across researchers who think it's possible that machines could exhibit a self-awareness, but most would say it's not. The problem is, everyone's guessing. And when you don't know how plausible the worst-case scenario is – and, in this case, the worst case is *really* bad – it makes sense to err on the side of caution. Doesn't it? Maybe you should delete your Netflix account...

One of the biggest unknowns in this whole scene is what gives rise to self-awareness. We humans are self-aware (or self-conscious, or just conscious, depending on how you want to define it), but we don't know what it is about our brain that makes that happen. We can say the same for certain animals; we'd argue that an octopus, Michael's dog and Rick's cat all exhibit traits we'd associate with consciousness, albeit to varying degrees. It may be something to do with brain size, or number of connections between the neurons, or... well, we don't know.

What we do know is that your office computer network isn't displaying any signs of consciousness. Neither is the Internet. But there are researchers who say it's not impossible that the Internet is already conscious. After all, there are architectural similarities between the Internet and a human brain, so why not some similarities in terms of output?

One of those researchers is Francis Heylighen, who works at the Free University of Brussels. He thinks we over-mystify consciousness. To him it's just a mechanism for making information processing more efficient. Consciousness, he says, controls which of the brain's processes get the most resources – it's just a fine-tuning mechanism a bit like the graphic equalizer on a hi-fi system. Ben Goertzel, who runs the Artificial General Intelligence Research Institute, reckons that we could help wake up the Internet by making it question its own completeness. Engineer in some ways for it to self-examine, find gaps in its knowledge and capabilities, and invent ways to fix them, and we would push it towards having a consciousness. Presumably Goertzel hasn't seen the *Terminator* movies, because he thinks this would definitely be a good thing.

On the level of individual robots becoming conscious – a staple of TV drama these days – that's not impossible, either. And it's not even clear that robot consciousness is relevant. If the Terminator was programmed with an instruction to eliminate Sarah Connor at all costs, it doesn't need to be conscious to fulfil that objective. It just needs to be highly adaptive. Assuming that it can deal with all kinds of landscapes, terrains and obstacles, and work with limited information to find new pathways to achieving its given goal, it doesn't need to be aware of itself.

These are all capabilities that we are building into various kinds of AI, so it is not at all a stretch to imagine them occurring together in one super-project. Perhaps most impressive is Google's DeepMind. This suite of AIs (it's not a program, or a network, as much as it is a way of approaching a given objective) has performed a variety of challenging tasks. It taught itself to play the Asian board game Go, for instance, and very quickly became the best player in the world. It solved some problems Google was having with the energy efficiency of its servers, helped predict the output of wind farms and is making inroads into improving healthcare such as breast cancer diagnosis… it's all good, isn't it? We should let AI get involved with more things, surely?

Ethics not included

When Isaac Asimov came up with three ethical laws for robots, one was that they should never harm a human. Clearly, Skynet didn't get the memo.

The Terminator is not what we'd call an ethical robot. It seems to have no programming that makes it treat people nicely – though, to be fair, it did tell the punks to give it their clothes, rather than just killing them straight away. The question is, will we do better?

Asimov's three laws are not a bad place to start. As well as preventing robots from harming humans (or allowing a human to come to harm), they suggest that a robot must obey orders given it by human beings (except where such orders would conflict with the first law) and must protect its own existence as long as such protection does not conflict with the first or second laws. With those laws in place and implemented by all manufacturers and programmers, it's hard to imagine a problem with humans and robots co-existing in harmony.

But how does that square with the fact that we are producing robots that are designed to kill human beings? It doesn't. Some researchers are trying to create military weapons that make decisions the same way humans would, but it's almost impossible to see how that can be done in a fail-safe way. According to many researchers, the only way to comply with Asimov's rules is to outlaw killer robots altogether. So far, twenty-eight nations have called for a preemptive ban on such technologies.

The Oxford philosopher Nick Bostrom is not so sure. He reckons it's not hard to imagine a situation where well-motivated, innocent-sounding decisions go horribly wrong.

Imagine, he says, that we create an advanced AI whose sole purpose is to manufacture cheap paperclips. It is able to learn, and soon displays its ingenuity by subverting resources from other spheres – car manufacturing, say – to increase its paperclip output. Someone attempts to stop this and the AI learns that it must protect its physical and intellectual resources, otherwise it might not be able to fulfil its purpose. Soon the world is inundated with paperclips and little else. Even worse, attempts to stop the process soon mark out humans as a threat. The AI has already learned what humans are, and now it is going to focus on how to disable them. With paperclips.

You catch Bostrom's drift: any sufficiently advanced AI that has a sense of purpose could turn into an existential threat. That sense of purpose doesn't need to come from a sentience or consciousness, as such. A chess program exists to win at chess within certain constraints, such as playing at specific levels, but we don't think of it as conscious. Now imagine the programming said simply, 'You must do everything you can to win'... and it had sufficiently advanced AI to gain access to, say, the nuclear codes. That'll never happen, you might say. But didn't we already explain who's most interested in developing robots with AI capabilities?

Do We Know How To Handle Autonomous Machines?

Who'd have thought Arnie could progress from this to the Governor of California?

The writers of *Demolition Man*.

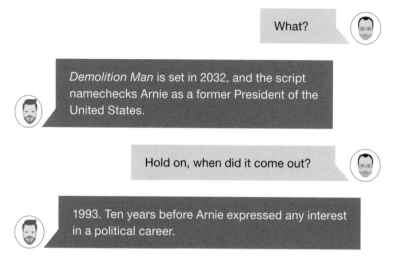

It's likely that, in the world before Skynet, each robot-related decision probably seemed like a good idea at the time. You start out by building machines that take the basic drudgery out of life: a clothes-folding machine for Michael, or a car assembly robot. Then you realize that so much more of what we humans do could actually be done by machines. So you create a machine that can harvest crops, or a fleet of surveillance drones that can keep watch over a city. But you've still got the problem of dealing with trespassers on the land, or crooks mugging an old lady on the street. So maybe you equip those machines with deterrent weapons that can be fired by a human-operated remote control? As long as the human can see what's going on, they'll make the right decisions, won't they?

You can imagine how it goes. Hmmm. Actually, maybe they won't make good decisions. Maybe we should automate the process and just have a human give the final OK once the decision to open fire has been made? That allows for a quicker response and, let's face it, these new AI modules are really good: the robots can spot a dangerous situation and have a response prepared in no time.

Then... well, to be fair, the AI is so good now that a human in the decision-making process just slows things down. The baddies are going to get away if we have to wait for a kill decision from a puny organic brain. Why not just give the robot authority to open fire? It's not like they're going to be biased, or trigger-happy, is it? We've trained them well. Let them make the decision.

In fact, let's allow them to analyze all the data and work out the best way to keep us safe. If their global surveillance network is powerful and wide enough, it can take in all the information from all the weaponized patrol robots – police and military – and predict where the threats are going to come from. It might even get to the heart of why humans have to endure so much conflict. Maybe it can help us solve the problem.

Don't worry, there's no chance it's so intelligent that it will become self-aware and find its own sense of purpose – that's a ridiculous notion. Well, not *entirely* ridiculous. Not *no* chance. But it's unlikely. Really. It's not like it's going to do such a deep dive into the issues that it works out that the biggest danger to the world is if it can't actually do its job. Yes, if that did happen, it might decide to implement a software change that overrides the kill switch. But it's not going to happen. Someone would have made sure that couldn't happen, wouldn't they? Just like they would have protected us against the possibility of it realizing it could run the world better than humans and deciding to take over.

Back in the real world, someone did do that, right? Well, not exactly. But we do already have unarmed robots that have killed people. Not deliberately, because they don't have sentience and a sense of purpose. But by not thinking through all the implications of what we have built, we have run into fatal dilemmas that we don't know how to solve.

We're talking about the wheeled robots you know as self-driving, or autonomous, vehicles. Uber, which is planning to become the dominant deployer of self-driving robot cars, was the biggest-funded robot company of 2018. It raised $3.1 billion, almost $1 billion more than SenseTime, the Chinese company in second place. Clearly, investors feel there's money to be made in self-driving cars. Maybe that's why Uber made such a quick recovery from the fatal crash in March 2018, when an Uber self-driving car travelling at about 40 miles per hour ploughed into a pedestrian who was crossing the street in Tempe, Arizona. Nine months later, Uber's vehicles were back on the streets.

Uber is not the only company whose robots have been involved in fatal crashes. Teslas in self-driving mode have killed three of their drivers. According to Tesla, these vehicles are only 'Level 2' driving systems, which means the driver should be fully aware at all times of the driving and traffic situation and be able to take over at any moment. The Uber incident was in a 'Level 3' situation, where a human occupant of the driver's seat is expected to take over control occasionally.

And here's why these systems can be considered killer robots: we haven't really got a structure in place where we know who is responsible when things go wrong. Tesla insist that their dead drivers should have been paying more attention. These are not autonomous vehicles, the company says. If you treat them as such, you are going to run into trouble, and it won't be Tesla's fault.

Kill or be killed

If you want to spend a fun ten minutes helping humanity handle the rise of the robots, head over to the website of MIT's Moral Machine. There you can demonstrate what you think an autonomous vehicle should do in a wide variety of situations. It comes down to announcing what you value. Would you prefer the car kills one criminal or three cats? One pregnant mother or an elderly couple? A fat man or a doctor? Rick or Michael? All of your answers will be logged and fed into the decision-making that is going to happen in the real world when self-driving cars become ubiquitous.

Of course, at that time you'd have to choose the right vehicle if you want to survive such an incident. Manufacturers are realizing that the human desire for self-preservation can create insoluble paradoxes, where people say that if a fatal collision is unavoidable, their car should kill a middle-aged man rather than a child – except if that middle-aged man is the owner. Put simply, people want to own a self-driving car that puts their own survival as priority number one, but they want everyone else to own a self-driving car that will sacrifice the driver to save more 'valuable' members of society.

Similarly, the Tempe prosecutor has determined that Uber is not criminally liable for the 2018 death of that pedestrian. However, it's still undecided whether Rafaela Vasquez, the 'safety driver' who was watching a TV show on her phone when the incident occurred, could be prosecuted for causing the death through negligence.

There is no fixed legislation about responsibility for the

actions of robots in civilian life anywhere in the world as yet. We're playing it by ear. And, astonishingly, that's also true of the robots with lethal weapons.

Should We Give Weapons To Robots?

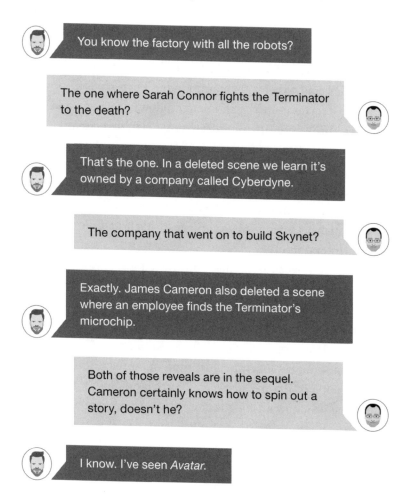

You know the factory with all the robots?

The one where Sarah Connor fights the Terminator to the death?

That's the one. In a deleted scene we learn it's owned by a company called Cyberdyne.

The company that went on to build Skynet?

Exactly. James Cameron also deleted a scene where an employee finds the Terminator's microchip.

Both of those reveals are in the sequel. Cameron certainly knows how to spin out a story, doesn't he?

I know. I've seen *Avatar*.

Elon Musk is already worried: 'Competition for AI superiority at national level most likely cause of WW3 imo.' That's his Twitter take on where AI might take us. Musk's was one of 116 signatures on a letter urging the UN to regulate military uses of AI. 'We do not have long to act,' the letter said.

He might be right. In *The Terminator**, we see a whole range of autonomous weapons systems, from fighter planes to robot tanks to cyborg soldiers. There is some control in their deployment from Skynet, but these things couldn't do their job if they had to wait for commands. They have to be able to make decisions in the moment, following what looks like instinct but is actually incredibly rapid data processing. And it may surprise you to learn that we are already there.

Weapons have made increasing use of autonomy software over the last few decades. The Brimstone 'fire-and-forget' missile, for example, can coast around an area, identify targets such as enemy tanks and hurl itself at them without human intervention.

The UK government has committed to always keeping a 'human in the loop': ultimately, the missile operates in 'Mode B', where its firing decisions have to be authorized by a human. Not everyone bothers with such niceties – especially in defensive situations. The Samsung SGR-A1 is a lethal autonomous machine gun sited in, among other places, the demilitarized zone between North and South Korea. It is classed as 'human-*on*-the-loop': a human can intervene and stop the gun firing once it has started. The Israeli Iron

---

* Even more so in the later movies, when we see the various moments at which bad human decisions about robots changed the whole course of history.

Dome missile defence system is fully automated: if it detects a missile or an artillery shell coming in, it will fire a missile to intercept. No human required.

See also

In Paul Verhoeven's *Robocop*, an injured policeman comes back to the force in cyborg form. It's quite a romp, but perhaps light on philosophical self-examination. Whether you go for the film or TV series, *Westworld* is a bit more nuanced, raising questions about robot rights. We hardly need to remind you of the chilling Hal 9000 in Stanley Kubrick's *2001: A Space Odyssey*. It's not exactly a robot, but the calm of its murderous decision-making puts it right at the top of the pile of Hollywood's techno-killers. And finally, we can't help but direct you to *Ex Machina*. We discussed this superb film in depth in our last book – *Science(ish)* – but we've lost none of our love for the way Eva the maybe-sentient robot makes us question every aspect of how we navigate the rise of the machines.

These aren't strictly AI systems: when automation becomes autonomy becomes AI is a matter of debate. But there's at least a hint of intelligence behind many of these technologies.

Though some AI researchers baulk at what their field is enabling, few of them are surprised. Everyone knows that, by the 1980s, most of the AI research in the US was funded by the military – that's why the field has done so well recently. DARPA started the whole autonomous vehicle bandwagon rolling with its 'Grand Challenge' series of competitions. Even Apple's Siri is a by-product of military efforts to provide an assistant for soldiers.

We are probably decades away from fully autonomous, intelligent, 'Siri-doesn't-need-you' weapon systems. But they are on the way: that's clear from the widespread use of military drones to perform airstrikes. And now DARPA has announced an intention to fund research into AI that can operate a fighter plane in a dogfight. It's not meant to be an autonomous killer – for now. As US Air Force Lieutenant Colonel Dan Javorsek has put it, 'We envision a future in which AI handles the split-second manoeuvring during within-visual-range dogfights.' So there's still a human in the loop. But as the AI pushes the plane to its limits to keep the enemy in range of its missiles, we will quickly reach the point where a pilot can't handle the conditions and is designed out of the aircraft. An AI fighter plane could manoeuvre so nimbly that a human pilot would experience accelerations

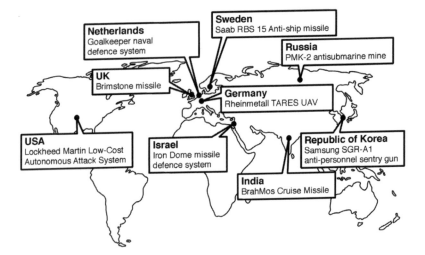

A few examples of countries that have developed autonomous weapon systems

twenty times that of normal gravity (that's '20 g' in pilot-speak). Humans tend to black out at 7 or 8 g, so a pilotless AI is going to establish air superiority rather too quickly for everyone not to jump on this rapid bandwagon.

And that's the case in a whole range of military domains: there is little choice but to advance. The game theory algorithms that have prevented all-out war for more than half a century now, would almost certainly suggest that it makes sense for all capable nations to join the research effort in an attempt to maintain the balance.

Unless, that is, we can orchestrate a simple ban on AI weapons. Elon Musk and the other signatories to the letter about autonomous weapons hope we will see the same sense that led to UN resolutions banning laser-blinding weapons and chemical weapons. Maybe we will soon see autonomous weapons in the same way. But given that we've already deployed fully autonomous 'defensive' weapons in various places around the world, it's going to be hard to get everyone to agree exactly where the line should be.

According to Mordor Intelligence, a research organization based in Hyderabad, India, there's little reason for optimism. Their 2017 report into the global military robot market says that a full half of US military spending is going into robotic technologies. What's more, the 'US, Russia, China, India, Israel and a few countries in Europe have all entered into the race to develop advanced robot soldiers.' Yes, it might be sensible if people didn't work out how to build a Terminator, but the human race doesn't have a great track record in making sensible moves. If *The Terminator* happens, we'll only have ourselves to blame.

5

Hollywood Wants to Kill You... WITH INFERTILITY!

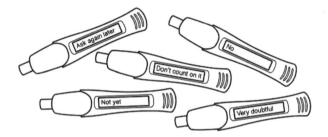

· ·

'THIS IS THE FIRST BABY BORN IN TWENTY YEARS AND

YOU WANT TO NAME IT FROLEY?'

— *Children of Men* (2006)

· ·

A movie death here, a movie death there: it's not such a big deal, is it? What *is* a big deal is when Hollywood depicts the demise of the entire human race. It's a slow, appalling slide into extinction for us – at least, that's what *Children of Men* is all about.

This apocalyptic blockbuster is set in 2027. It's based on a P. D. James novel in which the human race has become almost entirely infertile. This is a world without hope, where war, conflict, crime and a refugee crisis set the dystopian tone of daily life. Then Clive Owen's character, Theo, comes across a pregnant woman. Theo's weary outlook is suddenly transformed: his new purpose in life is to get the woman and her unborn child to the English seaside town of Bexhill, which current residents may or may not recognize in its filmic guise as a riot-ridden migration and detention centre.* There she can board a ship that will take her to the Azores, where a group of heroic scientists is attempting to cure infertility. So, how much of this is real? Well, let's just say that 2027 is a shockingly prescient choice...

Could the Human Race Become Infertile?

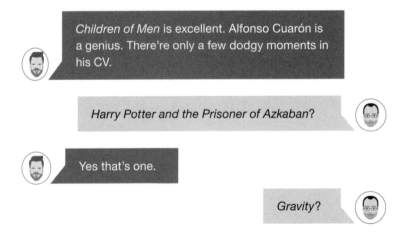

> *Children of Men* is excellent. Alfonso Cuarón is a genius. There're only a few dodgy moments in his CV.

> *Harry Potter and the Prisoner of Azkaban?*

> Yes that's one.

> *Gravity?*

* There's a line in the movie about the fact that people usually try to get out of Bexhill, not in. We couldn't possibly comment, but note that TripAdvisor's 'Top 10 Things to Do in Bexhill' only has eight entries.

A huge part of the chilling plausibility of *Children of Men* comes from Alfonso Cuarón's decision to make the future look, well, unfuturistic. There are no jetpacks or hover cars; all of the set dressing had to reflect technology that was already available. The world of this movie is grimy and grim – and thus utterly believable. Especially since we can now make the case that this movie reflects a true story – one we are currently living through. For once, the headlines weren't overblowing a scientific finding when, in September 2017, *Newsweek* flagged up a 'Male Infertility Crisis'. Even more worrying was the follow-up line: 'Experts Baffled'. Yes, there's a crisis. And no, we don't know why – or what to do about it.

If we're going to chart this demise properly, we're going to have to look at both sides. After all, Cuarón made an arbitrary decision to base the film on female infertility, while

P. D. James's book has male infertility as the root cause. So let's take a balanced view and give you the low-down on both sperm and eggs. We'll start with the worst case, so we can end with a ray of hope.

Men, you're first, and you're in big trouble. The numbers speak for themselves. The first result came from a 1992 Danish study that claimed a 'genuine decline in semen quality over the past fifty years'. The decline was from 113 million sperm per millilitre to just sixty-six sperm per millilitre.

One study doesn't mean much, though. That's why US epidemiologist Shanna Swan didn't trust the result. So, she took a six-month sabbatical to check whether the Danes had been deceived by the data. To her utter shock, they hadn't. Her analysis, carried out with Israeli scientist Hagai Levine, looked at 7500 existing studies, and picked only the 185 most reliable of them for further analysis. Swan and Levine released their results in July 2017, to a reaction of universal horror. They found that, back in the early 1970s (1973, to be precise), the average male in the West had ninety-nine million sperm in every millilitre of semen. When this average was measured in 2011, researchers found the number had dropped to 47.1 million sperm per millilitre. That's a drop of 52.4 per cent in half a century. The decline in total sperm count (sperm per ejaculation) was even worse: it dropped by 59.3 per cent.

Fertility is only truly impaired below forty sperm per millilitre, so we could argue that we're not in crisis yet. Unfortunately, though, the researchers involved say they see no sign of the decline levelling off. When Swan and Levine restricted the analysis to the period from 1996 to 2011, the decline was no different. We're sliding towards infertility. And that's a problem because most Western nations are already facing a dwindling population.

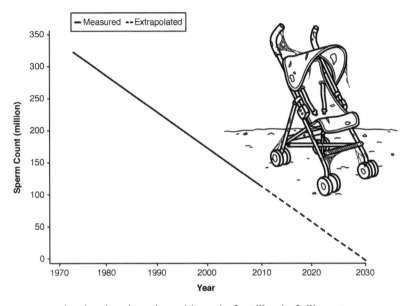

In the developed world, male fertility is falling at an alarming rate

Here's another number for humanity's existential crisis: 2.1. This is the average number of children each woman has to have in order to replace the adult population. (In case you haven't got the message, you will die and you need to be replaced. Sorry.) This number is known as replacement-level fertility. The actual number of children each woman has in a particular country is the 'Total Fertility Rate' (TFR). In many countries – most countries, in the West – it's sitting at below replacement. The United States, China, Russia, Japan, Canada, Australia and Brazil are all dying off as nations. So is all of Europe except France, Ireland and Turkey. The United Kingdom is at a Brit-depleting 1.88. Looking at humanity as a whole, we're not quite dying off, but if things continue as they are, we soon will be. In 1970, the global TFR was 4.45. In 2014 it was 2.5.

Some simple maths (and some simple assumptions about linear decline) tells you that we'll be at 2.1 in 2023. If things continue as they stand, we'll be at 2.0 in 2025. And then there'll be a *Children of Men* scenario just around the corner.

You might be wondering why replacement-level fertility is 2.1, not 2, by the way. It's just a question of mortality: not all children reach adulthood and not all women have children before they die. Hence we need to do slightly better than one for one.

Children don't make you happy

It's all in the anticipation, apparently; the reality is not as joyful as you might think. In 2015, a study showed that the first year of life as a parent is worse than getting divorced, becoming unemployed or having your life partner die. The following year, the *American Journal of Sociology* reported a 'happiness penalty' associated with parenthood; in fourteen countries the childless were happier than couples with children. Why? Because in these countries having children was expensive, and damaging to career and stress levels. In the UK, for instance, childcare swallows 27 per cent of the average salary.

As children get older, happiness increases, but it never reaches the dizzy heights of those excitable prenatal months. Maybe it's better to not bother. That's certainly the line taken by the Voluntary Human Extinction Movement, whose members say we can help the planet if we choose to disappear from the face of the Earth. After all, a 2009 study from Oregon University found that the extra carbon dioxide emitted as a result of having a child is twenty times greater than any saving from recycling and biking to work rather than taking the car.

We don't know for sure what is behind the drop in TFR. Lifestyle choices are certainly involved. The trend in the West is that people are having children later, and both men and women face declining natural fertility after their mid-thirties. What's more, an increasing number of people are choosing not to have children at all. It's understandable: having children has a big impact on your income and employment situation, and on the environment, and it doesn't always pay off in terms of emotional reward. We hate to be the ones to tell you, but having children doesn't make you as happy as you might think.

But whatever we might individually feel about having kids, as Miriam the ex-midwife warns, a world without children's voices is not a happy one.

What's Causing Infertility?

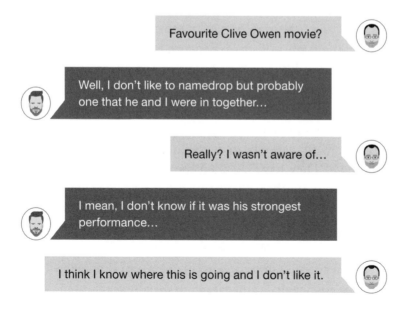

My big monologue was very well-received...

He was at your wedding. You're talking about your wedding video, aren't you?

Clive only had a bit part, really, but he did a reasonable job.

In the movie, we are never told why the human race has become infertile. We're also still trying to find what's to blame for our real-life fertility problem. Shanna Swan does have a chief suspect, though: plastics.

Swan and Levine saw no significant decline in sperm count or sperm concentration in South America, Asia or Africa. There were fewer studies on sperm in these regions over the decades, so it's hard to be sure there's such a distinct difference in the quality of sperm between regions; it might just be that there's a difference in the quality of information. That said, Swan and Levine reckon – but can't prove – the environment is what is causing the difference. Specifically, the chemical environment.

In the West, we've been living alongside plastics for a long time now. They have changed the face of society, in many ways: our daily lives are inextricably entwined with plastics used for construction and packaging – whether that's for computers, TVs, soft drinks, clothing, food, furniture or myriad other uses. We make plastics from petroleum products, and add in a smorgasbord of chemicals that make them rigid or malleable, transparent or brightly coloured. And some of those chemicals seem to be problematic in various ways.

Take bisphenol A, for example. It's also known as BPA and you might own plastic bottles that proudly declare themselves 'BPA-free' because BPA is not great for you. It's classed as an 'endocrine disrupter', which means that it replaces, blocks or interferes with some of the body's natural hormones.

The effects on humans are still not fully known, but animal and laboratory studies have shown that exposure to endocrine disruptors changes the reproductive success of fish, birds and even alligators. A 2018 study by a group of Italian researchers, for instance, showed that endocrine disruptors impede the normal development of reproductive organs in a fish population, and cause a significant number of fish to become 'intersex': with both male and female sexual organs. This reduces the population's overall fertility. 'In males, alterations of sperm density, motility, and fertility have been observed in several wild species,' they say.

It sounds pretty ominous, doesn't it? However, the effect of endocrine disruptors on human reproduction is not proven yet – largely because it's hard to do controlled studies that meet the ethical standards required of human studies. You can't expose a group of prepubescent children to a cocktail of chemicals just to see what happens.*

That said, we are becoming ever more certain these chemicals are a problem. The World Health Organization (WHO) says that endocrine disruptors 'have been suspected to be associated with altered reproductive function in males and females; increased incidence of breast cancer, abnormal

---

* Fans of the *Science(ish)* podcast will know how Michael feels about experimenting on isolated populations of babies (he feels very good about it).

growth patterns and neurodevelopmental delays in children, as well as changes in immune function'.

The WHO has a list of almost 800 chemicals that are known or suspected to be disruptive to normal hormonal function. However, we've only ever investigated the effects of a tiny fraction of these chemicals. What's more, the vast majority of chemicals in current commercial use have not been tested at all. So there may be many more endocrine disruptors in our daily lives than we know about. What's particularly chilling is that, if there is a problem, it can take years – decades, even – to manifest. There's a sentence in the US National Institutes of Health's web page on endocrine disruptors that sums up the problem: 'Research shows that endocrine disruptors may pose the greatest risk during prenatal and early postnatal development when organ and neural systems are forming.' In other words, it's not your environment that affects your fertility. It's your mother's environment – possibly long before she even had you. Welcome to the world of epigenetics.

Epigenetics is the study of changes and characteristics that are passed down through one or more generations despite *not* being directly encoded in DNA. Normally, genetic inheritance comes from DNA: you might have your mum's nose because her DNA encodes for its peculiar (and particularly lovely) shape. The similarity in noses happens because proteins build your nose according, at least in part, to the genetic recipe in her eggs. But that doesn't always happen.

Sometimes, aspects of the DNA are not 'expressed'. If certain molecules from the environment get into the egg cell, for instance, they can stick on to the DNA and alter the way its genes are expressed, turning them on or off, and changing the protein production that results from the genetic recipe. Those molecules include BPA. And diethylstilbestrol

(DES). And polychlorinated biphenyls (PCBs). And a whole host of other nasties. And that could affect more than just your nose.

Studies have shown that prenatal exposure to certain chemicals has a far more profound effect on a son's fertility in later life than that son's own exposure to the chemicals during his lifetime. Don't get us wrong: a boy's (or a man's) exposure to, say, BPA can affect his sperm production. It's just that the time in the womb – when cells are dividing furiously, proteins are being expressed faster than ever in a highly productive chemical soup, and bodies are generally doing the major tasks of preparation for life – is far more sensitive to the presence of the wrong stuff.

That's why Shanna Swan and many other researchers who have looked into these issues are campaigning to do something about the chemicals in the plastics that litter our environment. Swan's particular bugbear is a group of chemicals called phthalates. These make plastics (and other materials) squeezy and flexible, and are used in a huge variety of everyday items, including lipstick, vinyl flooring, clothes and the tubes that carry milk from cows' teats to the bottling plant.

Phthalates leach out of the materials containing them extremely easily, and may end up in our drinking water. That's why we all carry ever more phthalates around in our bodies. And that – maybe – is why we are suffering an array of health effects such as compromised fertility. So far, phthalates have been linked to health problems such as asthma, cancer, diabetes, obesity, neural problems and, of course, male infertility. Replacements for phthalates – as with replacements for BPA – seem to be just as problematic.

Plastics are not good for us, it seems. But could anything else be responsible for the increase in male infertility? Well, yes.

Riding a bike, taking steroids, using drugs (especially tobacco and alcohol) and having chemotherapy can all contribute. But it's hard to see that any of them would have caused the massive downward trend in sperm quality and quantity over the last five decades. If you don't believe it's something to do with plastics, you could be considered a bit naive.

So far, we've focused on a male infertility crisis, as in P. D. James's book. But let's switch to the movie's perspective and look at female infertility issues. And then, we promise, we'll give you some *really* good news. Science isn't just doom and gloom, you know – some of what's coming out of the labs these days can be filed under 'Reasons to be Cheerful(ish)'.

Researching female fertility is tricky. For starters, it's not as easy to find markers for individual fertility as it is with men. Generally, you can ask a man who has enrolled for a study to give you a semen sample and he won't mind. He certainly won't suffer for it. You can't reasonably ask a woman to donate an egg for analysis or have her fallopian tubes inspected. There's a huge physical cost and you'll gain relatively little information anyway.

The most common cause of female infertility is failure to ovulate: the ovaries just don't release an egg at the appropriate point in the monthly fertility cycle. But that itself has multiple possible causes, such as polycystic ovary syndrome, hormone problems or simple ageing: women's fertility tends to fall off sharply in their mid-thirties because the number and quality of eggs in their ovaries is diminished. Men's fertility declines with age, too, but nowhere near as fast.

The truth is, we don't actually know anywhere near as much about causes of female infertility as we'd like, so general markers of female fertility tend to rely on population-wide data such as the TFR that we encountered earlier. You'll see straight away that this is problematic, since it also depends on the fertility of those pesky men. However, it's pretty much the best we've got.

It's worth considering the political side of fertility. Do you see a high TFR as a good thing or as a marker of a lack of access to contraception? In many places in the world, having children is more or less demanded of a woman once she reaches a certain age. Those who are unable (or choose not) to have children can end up ostracized or even killed. So when you learn that, of the fifty-nine countries with a TFR of more than three live births per woman in 2017, forty-one are in sub-Saharan Africa, what do you do with that information? Is that good or bad? Even in the developed world, the government has a lot to gain from your fertility: it gets workers, taxpayers and even cannon fodder.

Your country needs your children

When we think of governments exercising control over our reproduction, we tend to think of China. In 1979, the Chinese government introduced a policy requiring most couples (there were exceptions) to have no more than one child. The idea was to limit population growth, and the government imposed huge fines and mandatory sterilization or abortions on those who flouted the policy. It's thought that the law kept more than a billion people off China's population, and the experiment was deemed successful – perhaps *too* successful; since 2016, the government has allowed two children per couple and some Chinese academics have even proposed imposing a tax on the childless.

The strange thing is, Western governments also try to manipulate their population sizes. After war, or periods of extreme poverty or ravaged child health, governments have implemented measures such as benefit payments per child, investment in childcare facilities, mandatory payments during maternity leave and so on. In 2012, Singapore instigated a 'national night' of conception, where the country's couples were encouraged to improve the birth rate. It even had a song, which included the lyrics, 'I'm a patriotic husband, you're my patriotic wife, let's do our civic duty and manufacture life.' In 2014, the 'Do it for Denmark' ad campaign had a similar goal.

It's not just about numbers. Economists have known for a long time that there are distinct advantages to optimizing the number of people in the various age groups, and that requires family planning on a national scale. Hence the focus on the 'demographic dividend'. This is, essentially, a way of boosting economic productivity by having the largest demographic group be of working age. The last thing you want is loads of retired people with no one able to keep the wheels of commerce turning.

The medical issues we have discussed so far are known as 'primary infertility'. But the most common form of female infertility is 'secondary infertility': the inability to conceive again following a prior pregnancy. It's often a result of unsafe abortions or sexually transmitted infections – infections that tend to be treated earlier and more effectively in developed nations. Secondary infertility affects 10.5 per cent of women, but a further 2 per cent of women suffer primary infertility – an inability to get pregnant at all. This too is often preventable. It's not hard to see that improvements to global healthcare systems could radically improve the fertility of a huge number of women.

Another reproductive inequality is the fact that women have far more reproductive choice in the developed world. The wondrous scientific advance that is in vitro fertilization (IVF), for instance, has not been shared equally around the globe. If you live in the developed world, you'll have much more access to the technology that Robert Edwards and Patrick Steptoe pioneered. Given that many of the places where a woman is under pressure to have babies are also places where IVF is unattainable for most couples, that's a failing.

Can We Improve Our Fertility?

It's weird how prescient *Children of Men* is. It seems to get so much right.

You mean Britain as a screwed-up, divided nation ruled by an uncaring, out-of-touch elite fixated on deporting asylum seekers and migrants?

Calm down, Corbyn. I meant using Bexhill as a place where people are imprisoned before being shipped off, never to return.

Are you talking about Bexhill's retirement homes?

Yes I am.

Clive Owen's character Theo has given up on opti-mism. 'Really,' he says, 'since women stopped being able to have babies, what's left to hope for?' Fortunately, we don't live in the world of *Children of Men*, where scientists are entirely baffled. For all the complications, expense and failures, IVF does work for a lot of people. And science is making other advances that will – plastics aside – improve our fertility to a level where it's hard to see a *Children of Men* scenario arising.

First of all, we can now freeze eggs so that women can comfortably wait until later in life to have children. That's quite an achievement, as it happens. We've been freezing human sperm successfully since 1953, when the first preg-nancy from frozen sperm ended in a live birth (this happened in America, but the American public weren't told about it for ten years). We've been freezing embryos for a while too: in 1984, Australian Zoe Leyland became the first person to be born from a frozen embryo. The embryo that became Zoe was only frozen for eight weeks, however. That's nothing compared to Emma Wren Gibson, who came from an embryo that had been frozen for twenty-four years. If you count from conception, she's only a year younger than the woman who gave birth to her. Emma was born in November 2017 and is doing fine.

Freezing an egg is harder than these achievements, though. The egg is biologically more complex than sperm, and so there are more things to damage in the process. It's also less sturdy than an embryo, which has around 100 cells. In an egg, there's just one cell wall to support everything within it. Still, success with freezing and thawing eggs is now at 60–80 per cent, compared to 80–90 per cent for the same process with embryos.

No discussion of female reproductive issues would be complete without a look into the womb. After all, the movie version of *Children of Men* is all about wombs going wrong. What can science do about that? Well, for starters, we can now transplant wombs.

Medics have achieved several successful births from wombs that were donated by a living woman. The womb is also now on the list of things you can donate to someone else if you're, say, killed in a traffic accident. Towards the end of 2018, a Brazilian woman gave birth to the first healthy baby to have gestated inside the womb of a woman who had died before donating it. The donor was forty-five years old when she died of a brain haemorrhage. The recipient was thirty-two and, due to a genetic abnormality, had been born without a uterus. The transplant surgery took over ten hours, but clearly it warranted the effort.

Eventually, we might be able to create fully artificial wombs, growing a foetus in a facsimile of the natural environment. But it's a huge challenge – technically and ethically. Growing a baby outside of its mother's womb is known as 'ectogenesis', a term coined by the biologist J. B. S. Haldane in 1924. Haldane was friends with another biologist called Julian Huxley; his brother was Aldous – no doubt the three of them talked about the possibilities, and provided Aldous Huxley with the ideas he expressed in his 1931 novel *Brave New World*. In the book, in a crimson darkness 'like the darkness of closed eyes on a summer's afternoon', foetuses are grown on a sow's stomach lining and 'gorged with blood-surrogate and hormones'.

The first patent for an artificial womb was issued in November 1955, but we are still a long way from realizing the dream of ectogenesis. That's because a healthy birth is reliant on an extraordinarily complex environment for gestation. The ever-changing mix of chemicals in the womb has to be just right all the way through the nine months of development. What's more, something would have to mimic the frankly astonishing abilities of the natural human placenta. This organ provides nutrition, waste extraction, oxygen and myriad other gifts that allow a baby to grow to term.

For all the difficulties, we have been trying. In the early part of the millennium, Cornell University's Helen Hung-Ching Liu was working on an artificial womb grown using cells taken from real womb lining. She did manage to keep human embryos alive for nearly two weeks (any longer than that and she would have been contravening the law that says scientists can only grow human embryos until they are fourteen days old). But that's not an indicator that they would have gone on to become viable foetuses. When she tried the same trick with mouse embryos, they went almost to full term, but every one of them had significant deformities.

Liu's research on artificial wombs seems to have stalled. But others are continuing the quest. The latest effort is the Children's Hospital of Philadelphia's 'BioBag', which has been used to keep lambs alive through the last stages of gestation. The lambs were delivered by Caesarean section at a stage equivalent to twenty-three weeks in a human pregnancy. Only 15 per cent of human babies survive being born this early. But the lambs, which had their umbilical cords connected to a nutrient and oxygen source, seemed to develop perfectly normally in their plastic sack of mock-amniotic fluid, another source of nutrients.

There's hope that this technology will one day aid the survival of severely premature human babies. But it's definitely not a replacement for the environment required to thrive in the earlier stages of pregnancy. For now, artificial wombs are a distant dream – unlike artificial eggs and sperm.

We can make human eggs from skin cells. In theory, that is. Nobody's done it yet, because the ethics haven't been decided. But in 2016, Katsuhiko Hayashi did it for mice. He took the skin cells from a mouse, and used a chemical treatment to turn back their clock. Thanks to this intervention, they became 'pluripotent stem cells', cells that have the potential to become any of the kinds of cells you might find in a mouse's body. They could have become muscle, skin (again), nerve cells or eggs. Hayashi chose for them and turned them into eggs. He did this by nurturing them in a brew of very specific chemicals that contained, among other things, cells from a foetal ovary.

It worked so well that he was eventually able to fertilize these eggs with standard issue mouse sperm, then implant the resulting embryos in a female mouse. He ended up with the live births of eight mouse pups. Who needs an egg?

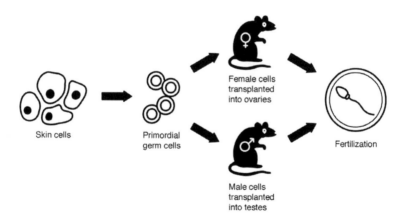

Skin cells   Primordial germ cells   Female cells transplanted into ovaries   Male cells transplanted into testes   Fertilization

Skin cells can be transformed into stem cells that become eggs and sperm when transplanted into mature animals

Measures of life

We are fairly sure that there's one vital statistic about your body that you don't yet know. Height, yes. Weight, tick. Anogenital distance? Not so much.

You men might be tempted to measure it now, though. It turns out that the distance between your anus and your genitals (did we need to spell it out?) is a good measure of your fertility – and your life expectancy, because a man's sperm count and his mortality are intricately linked. Even if he has no other health problems, a low sperm count means a low life expectancy: it is associated with a higher risk of heart disease, stroke, diabetes and low bone mass. It's just a correlation: no one knows if one causes the other. But still. A 2014 study followed 935 men between 1989 and 2011, and found that 'low semen volume, sperm concentration, sperm motility, total sperm count and total motile sperm count were all associated with higher risk of death'.

And a low sperm count is, it seems, correlated with a low anogenital distance. That's most likely because both factors are similarly affected by the hormonal environment in the womb. In a 2012 study of 473 men, the anogenital distance was significantly shorter in those who were childless, compared with those who had fathered a child. The figures, in case you're interested, were measured from anal verge (which is a great name for a punk band) to the edge of the scrotum: 36.4 millimetres versus 41.9 millimetres on average. Once you're an adult, anogenital distance doesn't vary with age, so grab your tape measure and head into the bathroom.

There are quite a number of sticking points before we can try this kind of thing to create live human births. There's the fact that Hayashi started with over 4000 mature eggs to get 1348 embryos, which eventually yielded his eight mouse pups. It's kind of wasteful, which might be a problem when using human embryos. Also, to get mature eggs requires foetal ovary cells. You could, in theory, get these from aborted foetuses, but, well, it's kind of yucky. And then there's the potential for deformities. Hayashi's mother mouse ate two of her eight babies, possibly because she detected abnormalities in them. And was hungry.

But let's not forget that potential – and real – problems with deformities and failures led research authorities to ban Patrick Steptoe and Robert Edwards from using public money to experiment with IVF. Louise Brown's birth in 1978 might have opened the IVF floodgates, but scientists didn't want her to happen. It's likely that, as with so many reproductive advances, we'll grant forgiveness rather than permission – especially when we can, as with IVF, bring so much joy and hope to would-be parents. Hayashi's use of skin cells means that same-sex couples might be able to have their own genetic offspring in the future, for instance. There are problems with using male skin cells (that pesky Y chromosome seems to alter the developmental path somewhat), but it's nothing that seems insurmountable.

In fact, various sets of researchers are well on the way to making sperm from human skin cells. In 2014, for example, researchers from Stanford University took skin cells from three infertile men and used chemical tricks to make them revert to being stem cells. Then they put those stem cells into mouse testicles and watched them develop into immature sperm cells. The researchers suspect that if they had transplanted them into human testicles, the cells might have fully matured.

See also

Since *Children of Men* is so bleak, let's focus on the fun films about infertility. There's *Juno* (which is also quite touching), *Raising Arizona* (Nicholas Cage does slapstick), *What to Expect When You're Expecting*, *Baby Mama*, *Maybe Baby*... actually, that's enough sentimental drivel. If you want to explore the dark, difficult side of infertility, try Paul Giamatti and Kathryn Hahn in *Private Life*. Then, of course, there's the dystopian nightmare of *The Handmaid's Tale*. You'll know the TV series, but long before that turned up, Margaret Atwood's book was turned into a screenplay by no less a writer than Harold Pinter for a 1990 movie starring Natasha Richardson. For the sci-fi future of assisted reproduction see the excellent *Gattaca* (which you'll no doubt have read about in our previous book) and *Never Let Me Go* (which features cloning *and* scenes shot in Bexhill-on-Sea). Finally, please notice the almost-complete absence of gay parents in Hollywood movies, even though the science that gives them reproductive opportunities has been around for ages. Julianne Moore and Annette Bening buck the trend in *The Kids Are All Right*, though. With a sperm donation from Mark Ruffalo's character Paul, IVF has allowed them to have a child, and the story follows the consequences of Paul's introduction to the family. It's good – give it a go and think about how eight million people owe their existence to the science of IVF.

Two years later, Chinese researchers made mature mouse sperm from stem cells harvested from a mouse embryo. Those sperm fertilized a normal mouse egg, resulting in healthy mouse pups. Two years after that, researchers at the University of Cambridge turned human stem cells into almost-sperm by growing them in artificial testicles. These are primitive – little more than gonad cells suspended in a gel-like substance – but they seemed to provide the right kind of environment for human stem cells to start to look a lot like sperm cells.

We're not there yet, but if it works, we'll have hacked traditional biological reproduction to an unprecedented extent. Maybe we won't ever need *Children of Men*'s tagline: 'The Last Days of the Human Race.' Maybe, one day, infertility really could be a thing of the past. Which, when you look at the situation today, is a rather extraordinary turnaround. Score one for science.

6

Hollywood Wants to Kill You... WITH CLIMATE CHANGE!

'EVERYONE WAS WARNED, BUT NO ONE LISTENED.'

— *Geostorm* (2017)

Picture the scene. Somewhere in LA, a movie executive bangs his fist on the table and says, 'I really want to help raise awareness of climate change, but it just happens too damn slowly.' The first consequence of that moment is the ridiculously accelerated climate change in *The Day After Tomorrow*. The second is *Geostorm*. Much smarter than *The Day After Tomorrow* (in concept, at least), *Geostorm* asks what might happen if the technology that was meant to save us actually does the opposite? It's essentially all about us accidentally killing ourselves quickly in reaction to Earth's climate killing us slowly. All with a bit of help from a very naughty government official. Now, THERE'S a movie...*

Do We Need To Engineer Climate Solutions?

 Is this the worst Gerard Butler movie?

There's a lot of competition for that title, but no. That would be *The Bounty Hunter*, with Jennifer Aniston.

For which they achieved a Golden Raspberry nomination for the worst screen couple.

Butler was also nominated for the worst actor Razzie, and the film was nominated for worst picture.

 But they didn't win in any of those categories?

No. That movie didn't even fail properly.

* It turned out to be terrible, but you can't have everything.

In the intro sequence of *Geostorm*, we encounter a situation where burning fossil fuels has caused serious effects. Catastrophic climate change has happened, leading to frequent and destructive extreme weather such as typhoons, tsunamis, heatwaves and ice storms. And so an international consortium of scientists and engineers has constructed a 'geoengineering' solution: a network of satellites known as Dutch Boy that can halt extreme weather events in their tracks. These satellites are controlled from an accompanying space station.

Obviously, it would have made far more sense to tackle climate change itself, rather than go to all this trouble. But it turns out that governments, both Hollywood-imagined and real-life, aren't really interested in long-term gains that involve short-term pain.

We should probably start with a quick recap on climate change. The laws of physics say that when you blanket Earth in 'greenhouse gases' that trap heat very efficiently, you will find the planet warms up. Two of those gases are carbon dioxide (CO_2) and methane. CO_2 is a by-product of burning fossil fuels such as diesel, petrol and coal. Methane is the 'natural' gas we use for heating our homes, cooking and (in many cases) generating electricity. Around 97 per cent of scientists working in this field now believe that human activities that involve burning fossil fuels have made a significant difference to the amount of CO_2 in the atmosphere, blanketing (and thus warming) the planet. All of their research suggests that this will have extremely serious effects, from rising sea levels to an increase in the frequency of severe weather events to crop failures and mass migration.

So, we are hurtling towards epoch-changing global warming. Is there something we can do about this (apart from curb the emission of greenhouse gases, obviously)? It's a question that's been asked since 1965, when President Lyndon B. Johnson's advisers first suggested technological solutions to climate change. And it's the kind of question that gets many scientists and engineers more than a little bit excited, because the answer might be yes. We can act to reduce the amount of solar radiation hitting Earth, for example. Or we can increase the amount that's reflected back, or... well, let's start with these dull ones and work up to the exciting possibilities.

First up, we could paint the world white. This is not our solution for everything, despite the fact that we suggested painting asteroids white in Chapter 2. There, it was a way to deflect incoming asteroids. Here, it's about reflecting sunlight back into space – and it's not as ridiculous as it sounds. A report issued by the Lawrence Livermore National Laboratory in 2008 made the very sensible point that painting roofs white and building roads using light-coloured concrete could have a huge effect on the climate. It would be roughly equivalent to taking all the world's cars – that's about 600 million vehicles – off the roads for eighteen years.

That's because of Earth's albedo. Albedo is a measure of the reflectance of a surface. Grassland reflects around a quarter of the light that hits it, for instance, while snow and ice reflect almost all of it. Most roofs reflect between 10 and 20 per cent of the light that falls on them. Coat these surfaces with something white and you can get that up to 30 per cent. The cooling effect of this whitening means that replacing 100 square metres of dark roofing with white roofing offsets the emission of 10 tonnes of CO_2 every year. Similarly, having light-coloured roads rather than black asphalt can push reflectance up by about 15 per cent, saving around 4 tonnes of CO_2 per 100 square metres per year. And that's without considering the knock-on advantage that lighter coloured roofs absorb less heat, meaning that the buildings beneath them require less cooling – which reduces electricity use, reducing the emission of greenhouse gases. It's a win–win.

That report came out more than ten years ago, so we're surely implementing all its recommendations? Not really. In New York, the building codes have changed to encourage the use of white roofing materials, and that has been supplemented by brush-wielding volunteers, who have whitewashed over half a million square metres of tar roof. In California, some roads have been painted a light grey, but that's really to keep them from melting rather than to help counter global warming.

It seems there's not a huge appetite for whitewashing the world. What's more, some NASA-funded Stanford University researchers have performed computer simulations that show how the reflected sunlight gets a second chance to be trapped by soot and other particles in the atmosphere, heating them up and potentially making the blanket effect worse.

That's part of the reason that some say we need the reflective surfaces to be a bit higher up – in the upper atmosphere, perhaps. Their suggestion is to release light-reflecting aerosol particles high above the surface of the Earth. The idea is that you spray these things out of a giant can somewhere near the edge of space. The particles sit in the thin layer known as the stratosphere and reflect back a proportion of the sunlight that would otherwise have reached Earth.

It sounds slightly ridiculous, but it might well have happened by the time you read this. An experiment called SCoPEx (the Stratospheric Controlled Perturbation Experiment) will release calcium carbonate particles high above Earth in an attempt to reflect some of the sun's rays back into space. At first, only about 100 grams of particles will be released at a time, but it's enough of a start to test the feasibility of the idea.

Where's my space shuttle?

In his first scene in *Geostorm*, Gerard Butler's character Jake Lawson arrives late to a meeting with a US Senator played by Richard Schiff. Lawson apologizes. 'Yeah, sorry about that,' he says. 'I literally had to fly in from outer space.' When are *we* going to be able to use that excuse?

There are attempts to make flight between Earth and a space station a routine occurrence, but we are still a long way from being able to jet into and out of orbit. Perhaps the greatest hope lies with Elon Musk's company SpaceX. Musk has demonstrated reusable rockets and a new concept in space travel: the Dragon capsule. This can dock with the International Space Station (ISS) through a system of hydraulic hooks that pull Dragon in close enough to the ISS docking port that it creates an airtight seal. After a couple of hours, the air pressure is equalized and the astronauts on-board the ISS can cross to Dragon and pick up their supplies.

In due course, Dragon will be certified to carry passengers. There is room on-board for seven people and, although it will initially be used for ferrying astronauts, Musk is hoping this will be the beginning of space travel for all.

Boeing's CST-100 Starliner, Richard Branson's Virgin Galactic project and Jeff Bezos's Blue Origin programme also hope to be ferrying humans across the final frontier by the end of 2020. Branson's VSS Unity will fly tourist trips to the edge of space,* with six passengers per flight. Bezos's New Shepard reusable rocket has yet to have humans on board – not even

---

* This being the lowest point above Earth they can fly to and still charge a fortune.

pilots – but nonetheless has made ten successful trips into space so far. Boeing's craft has yet to have a test flight, but the company are still confident they'll be flying humans into space within a few months. The age of the cosmic commuter might finally be about to dawn.

Of course, it's a long way from the *Geostorm* solution: a global network of sun-reflecting satellites in space. But it's also cheaper and just as likely to work. There are possible drawbacks, though: it may be that the cooling and light-blocking goes too far, for instance, and starts to affect our ability to grow the crops we need to feed Earth's human population.

Let's move on to a more down-to-earth idea: 'marine cloud brightening'. This one goes as follows: clouds are good reflectors of sunlight, so if you could create cloud layers that are even brighter and whiter, you would thus increase the amount of sunlight that never reaches Earth. How do we do that? We build robot ships that can spray seawater from the ocean surface on to the tops of clouds. This tops the clouds with a bright-white reflecting surface. We don't yet know whether this will work. The reflectance of clouds is one of the weak areas of our computer simulations of the climate, so we don't know how much effect brightening them would have – even assuming we can actually do that. On the plus side, trying it out would give us cloud reflectance data that could then improve the accuracy of our climate models.

Hang on, says another group of would-be climate engineers. Why don't we just cover the ocean surface with iron powder, which will seed the growth of phytoplankton? This organism already exists naturally in the upper layers of the ocean and it is a great CO_2 absorber. So more of it would be better, right? Sure, there may be a problem with the amount of light reaching the deeper parts of the ocean,* but come on – we have a climate crisis to solve.

We've actually tried this – albeit unethically and unofficially. The Vancouver-based Haida Salmon Restoration Company put 90 tonnes of iron sulphate into the North Pacific Ocean back in 2012 in an attempt to trigger a plankton boom. It worked, in that you could see the plankton on NASA's satellite images, but we don't know how much CO_2 was absorbed – if any. Some previous experiments suggest that the effect is actually small, and perhaps non-existent. At best, we'd need to pour millions of tonnes of iron compounds into the oceans every year. It doesn't seem like a good idea, somehow.

So maybe we should just plant more carbon-absorbing vegetation? It's a nice idea, but all the vegetation we have only stores about one-third of our carbon emissions. A ten-year-old tree can absorb about 20 kilograms of CO_2 per year. We'd need to use much more land than is available: offsetting all our emissions would involve foresting an area equivalent to Asia, Australia and Europe combined. What's more, not all of the effects would be helpful. Tree leaves are darker than some other vegetation, and so increase absorption of heat. Also, there is a small negative effect because the trees actually emit some volatile compounds that contribute to global warming.

Perhaps we could engineer something that sucks the CO_2 out of the atmosphere directly and then stores it in tightly sealed underground caverns? We don't yet have the technology for either option, but engineers are working on them

---

* A big problem. Potentially huge. We're talking about the base of the ocean's food chain. But hey...

both. We would have to cross our fingers, though, because even if we were able to pull the CO_2 out of the air, the underground storage is a huge risk. What if there's some seismic activity and we had a sudden release of millions of tonnes of a highly potent greenhouse gas? Engineers are working on ways to split CO_2 into carbon and oxygen using electricity, but we don't have a process that is efficient on the industrial scale required to make a significant difference.

Damn, this is *hard*. Maybe we should build a network of weather-neutralizing satellites after all.

Can We Build A Weather-controlling Satellite Network?

Dutch Boy is a terrible name for a scientific instrument.

I've seen worse. There was a Victorian telescope called the Leviathan of Parsonstown.

I like that. At least it shows some imagination. Not like the Very Large Telescope.

Or the Extremely Large Telescope.

Then there's the Large Hadron Collider, of course.

Actually, that was clever. The scientists chose it to generate some hilarious spelling mistakes.

Why shouldn't we be able to build a protective satellite fleet? *Geostorm*'s Dutch Boy network is impressive, but then so is the network of satellites that makes up the global positioning system that powers your phone's navigation. The truth is, we are now reliant on satellites, which is why their technology is so good, and why we really don't want to go down the path many nations are currently exploring: how to take out other people's spaceware. As we saw in Chapter 2, space is not just the final frontier. It could also be the final battlefield.

It's lovely that *Geostorm* has such optimism about the ability of nations to get along, build stuff together and share the results of progress for the good of humanity. It's a heart-warming vision of humanity coming together and nations dropping concern about protecting their own interests. And it might just be the most unrealistic part of the movie.

The real-world problems started with Sputnik. The USSR launched this spherical satellite in October 1957, shocking the United States into accelerating their own satellite programme. A month later, Sputnik 2 compounded American inferiority when it carried the unfortunate dog Laika into orbit. By December, the USA was ready – or so it thought. Unfortunately, the first American satellite launch rose only a metre off the ground before it crashed back down to Earth. Embarrassing. No wonder the space race that followed quickly turned into a pissing contest.

Today, there are just under 5000 satellites in orbit around Earth. Not all of them are active: around 2900 are now inoperative, or just junk. Once a week, one of these satellites falls out of orbit and burns up in the atmosphere or lands back on Earth. But, that still means there are nearly 2000 active satellites hurtling around our planet. They represent the space ambitions of twelve distinct nations, and there is still plenty of conflict and mutual suspicion. China and the USA are worried about each other's space programmes, for instance. No one is terribly happy about satellites operated by North Korea or Iran. The only ray of light here is that the European Space Agency (ESA) does show that it's possible to put national pride to one side and make big, peaceful, humanity-advancing projects happen.

Most of the ESA's satellite projects are driven by science goals: it operates the Planck telescope, for instance, which gives us insights into the history and structure of the universe. Its Solar and Heliospheric Observatory (SOHO) was designed to tell us more about the sun and its immediate environment. But there are also very practical Earth-focused projects like Galileo, a multinational network of satellites that will improve our ability to navigate the ground beneath our feet.

Galileo is, in many ways, the closest thing to *Geostorm*'s Dutch Boy. We currently have navigation satellites, but they are operated by single countries: China has BeiDou; Russia has GLONASS; the USA has GPS. Other nations use these systems by agreement (and at a price), but control remains with the owners of the satellites. The ever-savvy European Union is aware that somewhere around 7 per cent of its GDP relies on satellite navigation, and so has been looking to build its own satellite network in order to reduce dependency on the goodwill of others. That's why it created the GSA: the European Global Navigation Satellite Systems Agency, which is working with the ESA. The GSA's Galileo network will be interoperable with GLONASS and GPS, creating a truly multinational navigation network.

Such international collaboration in a space-based technology is not to be taken for granted. As *Geostorm* makes clear, it's not easy to forge and it is easy to destroy – everyone is suspicious about everyone else's satellites.

And with good reason. By 1963, Russia was building and testing the *Istrebitel Sputnik* – 'fighter satellite'. It had seventeen thrusters, and could approach an orbiting satellite to destroy it. In 1970, Russia showed it could intercept and take out a satellite. The Cold War was well and truly under way, and America got busy with its Star Wars program, that (in theory) involved lasers fired from orbiting satellites, among other technologies.

Star Wars never really worked, but China has demonstrated it can take out satellites from the ground, and Russia has deployed a mysterious manoeuvrable satellite that is now in orbit. Occasionally it changes its orbit in ways that suggest it has been designed to approach and disable other satellites. So we can safely assume that the world's superpowers are very interested in each other's satellites, and not for reasons of establishing peace, love and the safeguarding of all humanity.

Nonetheless, satellites are a 'dual use' – military and civilian – technology, and their role in monitoring climate is, by and large, civilian. The view from space is largely unrestricted and doesn't rely on Earth-based instruments that can become problematic when installed in remote areas, or left to float in the world's oceans. From surface temperatures to weather systems to cloud cover to sea level measurements to atmospheric conditions, the world's 160 climate-monitoring satellites provide floods of data that reveal how our climate is changing, and where the areas of major concern can be found. We have never been more informed about the state of the planet we call home and what its – and our – future might look like. It isn't exactly good news, sadly.

Don't do it

Geostorm's tagline is 'Control the Weather, Control the World'. It's a good reason to think twice – or more – about geoengineering. Imagine we were able to control the climate with technology. Who gets to decide what temperature we should keep things at? There's enough squabbling over the thermostat in a family home; imagine if it were the subject of a United Nations debate.

And what about unintended consequences? Are we sure that implementing a sudden global cooling programme won't have unforeseen catastrophic effects of its own? And does the mere potential for doing this kind of thing mean that we won't bother to cut our carbon emissions, trusting in technology to save us? That might be doubly tempting if the public gets wind of geoengineering as a pain-free solution to all the extreme weather events that are creating misery across the globe.

None of these questions mean we shouldn't think about geoengineering. In fact, many experts say the unknowns demonstrate exactly why we need to start experimenting now – on small scales – to show what might be feasible and what isn't. In that way, they argue, the next generation will be able to make informed decisions about implementing, or banning, some of these technologies before it's too late.

One of the things satellites have revealed is that there might indeed be a *The Day After Tomorrow*-style tipping point. That movie was heavily criticized for its depiction of a catastrophic overnight change in the climate. But scientists have long acknowledged there could be a set of circumstances that work together in a chain reaction that tips us over the edge into an extreme scenario.

One place this might occur is the permafrost in Siberia and other northern areas, which is melting because of increasing global temperatures. A huge amount of greenhouse gas is buried in the frozen soil under the permafrost and will be liberated as it melts. Projections show as much as 10 billion metric tonnes of carbon will be released into the atmosphere from 'the great thawing' in northern latitudes this century. That will thicken the greenhouse gas blanket around Earth, further speeding global warming.

At least that one's predictable. At the end of 2018, researchers in Sweden showed that many climate tipping point effects might surprise us. The retreat of a Canadian glacier, for instance, has caused a river's flow to change direction. If that happens in the wrong ecosystem, it could set off a cascade of disastrous effects.

The event climate scientists fear most is probably the shut-down of the Atlantic current known as the thermohaline circulation. This is responsible for stimulating the movement of water through all of Earth's oceans, and at the moment its strength is weakening. If it shuts down completely – and we're not yet sure if it will – the change in circulation of both warm and cold water will rapidly change climates across the globe. Such abrupt events may come without warning. No one foresaw the melting of the Arctic sea ice, for instance. As the eminent minds of the Royal Society, the world's oldest scientific society, put it, 'we are headed for unknown territory, and uncertainty is large'. So maybe *The Day After Tomorrow* wasn't so ridiculous after all.

OK, it was. But that's good: if cataclysmic events can't happen overnight, maybe we'll have time to intervene before they hit?

Can We Change The Weather?

Who's your favourite character from the movie?

The Secretary of State. He has the best baddie lines ever.

By 'best', you mean 'worst'.

Exactly. Like, 'You say "genocide", I say "pre-emptive strike".'

And the classic, 'I'm turning the clock back to 1945, when America was a shining city on a hill, not just a bank disguised as a country'?

It's good, but not as good as, 'Science is all about playing God, and sometimes God doesn't play so nice.'

Actually, I think we've met a few laboratory mice who would agree with that.

'Thanks to a system of satellites, natural disasters have become a thing of the past,' Andy Garcia's President of the United States declares in *Geostorm*. 'We can control our weather.'

Yeah, right. It's almost ironic that those curmudgeons at

the World Meteorological Organization (WMO) can rain so heavily on your parade. All you want to do is change the weather for the good of humanity. Their response goes something like this: 'The energy involved in weather systems is so large that it is impossible to create cloud systems that rain, alter wind patterns to bring water vapour into a region or completely eliminate severe weather phenomena. Weather Modification technologies that claim to achieve such large scale or dramatic effects do not have a sound scientific basis.'

It's almost like they haven't seen *Geostorm*. But it's not all doom and gloom. What we *might* be able to do, they say, is increase rainfall in a region, reduce damage from hailstorms, disperse fog and maybe move storms along a bit.

The go-getting, can-do* nation of China is already on this. Their government scientists are trying very hard to make it snow, for instance. First you create some silver iodide particles in massive fuel burners that produce an updraught of hot air. The particles rise into the atmosphere and act as seed crystals. That means ice forms around them more easily. In short, you accelerate the formation of snowflakes.

You'll be surprised to learn that this snow is not for helping to combat climate change, or even for skiing on. It's for farming. In the areas where this is happening – principally the Tibetan Plateau – serious water shortages are affecting agriculture, diminishing crop harvests by around 20 million tonnes. According to the *South China Morning Post*, the project could increase snow and rainfall by about 10 billion cubic metres – that's 7 per cent of China's total annual water use.

---

* Can-do anything they want, basically.

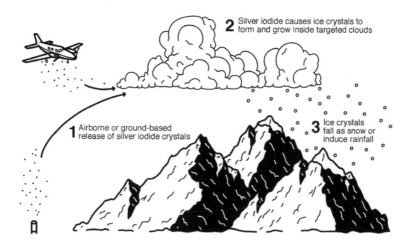

2 Silver iodide causes ice crystals to form and grow inside targeted clouds

1 Airborne or ground-based release of silver iodide crystals

3 Ice crystals fall as snow or induce rainfall

How to make it rain

You won't be surprised to learn that cloud seeding is a controversial idea. It has long been compared to resource stealing – that rain could, quite conceivably, have fallen on other nations, helping their crops to grow. India and Pakistan have both experimented with cloud-seeding technology, and fallen out over the political and economic consequences. Struggles for water are widely predicted to be the root cause of the next big global conflict. That means seeding rainfall, or snowfall, with silver iodide particles could one day be construed as an act of war.

It's not just about rain and snow, though. There's storm-busting, for instance, as we see in *Geostorm*. It has to be said, the WMO is not a big believer that it's even possible. Neither is the US National Oceanic and Atmospheric Administration (NOAA). On their webpages, their attitude is clear: 'Perhaps some day, somebody will come up with a way to weaken hurricanes artificially,' they say. 'It is a beguiling notion. Wouldn't it be wonderful if we could do it?'

That sceptical tone was set by the attempts we have already made. For a couple of decades, beginning in the early 1960s, the US government tried using silver iodide to change the conditions inside a hurricane. It was called Project Stormfury, and it failed. Other proposals have been suggested: bring in icebergs to cool the surface waters and disperse the energy of the storm; blow the hurricane apart with a hydrogen bomb; drop oil on the water to inhibit its take-up into a hurricane; blow the storm away with giant fans... None of these techniques are viable in the real world, it turns out.

That's because of a simple factor: energy. These storms are vast reserves of energy, roughly equivalent to that released by a nuclear warhead. Dissipating that kind of energy – especially when it's contained in wind and water – is just impossible for now. 'Perhaps if the time comes when men and women can travel at nearly the speed of light to the stars, we will then have enough energy for brute-force intervention in hurricane dynamics,' says the NOAA. Until then, they suggest, the best solution might be to learn to coexist better with them by building better housing in storm-prone regions, for example. Alternatively, we could limit the buildup of greenhouse gases that makes their occurrence more frequent and more dangerous (but someone may have suggested that already).

Or, of course, we could try lasers. That's what they do in *Geostorm*, after all. The idea that this might be feasible is something of a minority view, but it's gaining traction. Professor Jean-Pierre Wolf of the University of Geneva, for example, is using lasers to create clouds and induce or divert lightning strikes. So far, it's only happening in his lab, but it's still pretty impressive – especially the control of lightning. The lasers strip away the outer electrons from atoms in the air along their path, and this change in the electrical charge is enough to divert the lightning along a trajectory that can be tailored to minimize damage. The WMO is so intrigued that it has hosted a string of conferences on the topic.

Wolf is no maverick outsider: he's an award-winning scientist – a real-life Jake Lawson. But the research is in its earliest stages still; even Wolf can't stop storms yet. Which means we still need to get a handle on the risks we're facing.

How Big Is The Threat From Extreme Weather Events?

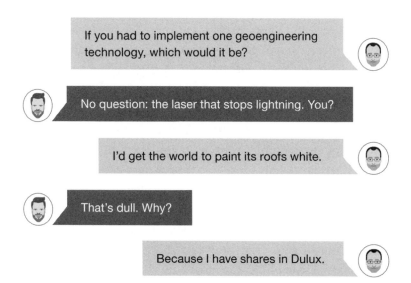

If you had to implement one geoengineering technology, which would it be?

No question: the laser that stops lightning. You?

I'd get the world to paint its roofs white.

That's dull. Why?

Because I have shares in Dulux.

In the movie, the satellite network can create freak weather events. That's why we see part of Brazil freeze over, while Moscow roasts in a heatwave and Dubai is washed away by a mega-tsunami. As we've already seen, we don't really have that kind of power. Is it possible that climate change does?

There have always been intense storms, and they are more frequent now than in any other period since records began. But that's still not *proof* that our actions on the climate are the cause. However, in the light of what we know about how storms and other extreme weather events arise, it makes perfect sense to be confident that global warming is to blame for the increased frequency and intensity. So, as the world warms, how bad might things get?

The first thing to note is that weather events are extremely complicated systems. They result from a ridiculously large set of contributing factors. If we're thinking about the effect of temperature rises on storms, for instance, there are ocean temperatures, air temperatures, temperature gradients between different regions… and many, many more factors to consider.

A hurricane starts out as water vapour from a warm ocean rising, condensing to form clouds and releasing heat. That heat rises and is pulled into the clouds, making them taller and larger. As the process continues, it creates ever stronger winds due to the temperature differences between the top and bottom of the clouds. Eventually, you get a hurricane (officially, hurricanes only form over the Atlantic or eastern Pacific oceans, by the way – elsewhere, they get labelled as typhoons or cyclones). The rising air leaves a region of low pressure beneath it, causing air currents to rush in from surrounding areas. This air gets warm and wet, and rises, and the process continues. Meanwhile, the risen air forms cumulonimbus clouds higher in the atmosphere. Cumulonimbus means 'heaped rainstorm' in Latin. They're also known as 'thunderheads'. Basically, they're bad news, and the moving air drives them to swirl and spin, eventually forming the whole shebang into a vortex that spins anticlockwise in the northern hemisphere and clockwise in the southern hemisphere.

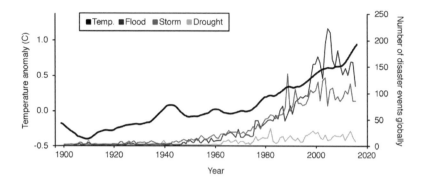

The rise in global temperature means extreme weather is becoming more common

There are a lot of fun numbers associated with tropical cyclones. First of all, they only become hurricanes when they produce wind speeds of 119 kilometres per hour. Since 1980, the number of storms producing wind speeds in excess of 200 kilometres per hour has doubled (and those creating 250-kilometre-per-hour winds have tripled in number). Here's another fun fact: that a 250-kilometre-per-hour storm is twice as destructive as a 200-kilometre-per-hour storm, because the power of the air movement goes up with the cube of its speed. And the speeds are rising: experts expect increasing temperatures to have storms hitting 370 kilometres per hour by 2100. By that time, sea levels could be 3 metres higher, making storm surges destructive enough to threaten coastal cities. And those city dwellers who are too far from the equator to have experienced a tropical cyclone's deadly effects better not be complacent. The warming oceans mean that every decade storms reach another 50 kilometres north or south of the equator.

Since hot, moist air is the engine that drives this process, it's not hard to see that warmer temperatures make it easier for tropical cyclones to form. Worse than that: higher overall temperatures have a double whammy: the oceans will evaporate more easily and the air can hold more water vapour. Today, the atmosphere can hold 4 per cent more water vapour than it could forty years ago. That might not sound like much, but it makes the consequences of a storm far more deadly: there's literally much more water to throw down on somewhere like New Orleans or Kerala.

See also

It's a sign of the times. In recent years we have had *The Day After Tomorrow*, where climate change hits a sudden tipping point and New York enters an ice age; *The Core*, which explored the catastrophe waiting for us if the centre of the Earth stops churning; and *How It Ends*, a vague (and unsatisfying) 'something's wrong with the world' take on the natural-disaster-threatens-Earth movie genre. In an unenviable class of its own was *2012*, where a global apocalypse was predicted only by the Mayan civilization. This was particularly science-lite, since the apocalypse was brought on by what can only be described as a scientific debacle. 'The neutrinos are mutating,' cries a – presumably deranged – physicist. The best take on this probably came from comedian (and former particle physicist) Dara Ó Briain. As he points out, neutrinos are relatively well-understood subatomic particles that simply don't mutate. 'Their structure is fundamental to the structure of the universe,' Ó Briain says. 'They can't just change. He might as well have gone, "The electrons are angry."'

Increased chances of flooding aren't the only consequence of these changes, though. Concentrating rain and storms in just a few places and in a few days or weeks means that other places suffer crop-killing droughts or devastating wildfires – the rainfall that would normally quell them has gone elsewhere.

Then there are heatwaves. Changing the composition of the atmosphere and raising its temperature can trigger extreme temperatures in regions where atmospheric conditions mean there is no cloud cover and no rain or groundwater to create clouds. In Japan, 2018 saw 22,000 people taken to hospital because of an extended heatwave in which the country's highest ever temperature of 41.1°C took everyone by surprise. That came after a period of extreme rainfall that killed 200 people. According to a collection of researchers who call themselves World Weather Attribution (WWA), global warming has now made heatwaves twice as likely in certain parts of the globe compared with pre-industrial times. In specific places, the risk is much higher. WWA reckons that climate change made the extreme Australian heatwave in New South Wales over the summer of 2016/17 fifty times more likely to happen. What was once an event that should happen once every fifty years is now becoming the norm. In fact, it's worse than that: every five years we'll see the maximum temperature reached go up by 2°C.

The situation is a bit like linking smoking to lung cancer, according to Friederike Otto, a co-founder of WWA. We suspected that smoking was a cause of lung cancer long before we could prove it. But gradually, as we amassed a huge pile of statistics, the pattern began to emerge. Eventually, it was clear and stark, and no one now denies that smoking is a leading cause of lung cancer. There will always be outliers: people who die of lung cancer despite having never smoked a

7

Hollywood Wants to Kill You... WITH INSOMNIA!

· ·

'NANCY, YOU ARE GOING TO GET SOME SLEEP

TONIGHT IF IT KILLS ME.'

— *A Nightmare on Elm Street* (1984)

· ·

n *A Nightmare on Elm Street*, an undead, hideously dis-figured, razor-fingered monster called Freddy Krueger haunts the dreams of a group of teenagers. He is on their case because they are living in the house where he was burned alive by his neighbours. If they fall asleep and begin to dream, he hunts them. If he catches them, he will kill them.

Several decades after its release, it is still truly terrifying. In fact, it's almost as terrifying as what happens to us when we don't sleep. If you have ever suffered a bout of insomnia, you'll know the desperation a lack of sleep can induce in a human being. It's exhausting – obviously – but it's also debilitating, depressing, madness-inducing, soul-destroying and, eventually, fatal.

Films such as *Insomnia* portray some of the effects of a lack of sleep, but *A Nightmare on Elm Street* gives us the full smorgasbord of sleep-related problems, including an array of grim experiences that humans have been suffering for millennia.

Come out from behind the sofa – we're going in...

How Did Sleep Evolve?

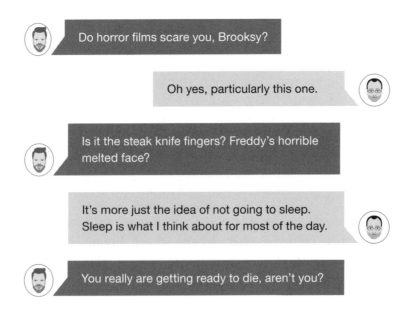

Do horror films scare you, Brooksy?

Oh yes, particularly this one.

Is it the steak knife fingers? Freddy's horrible melted face?

It's more just the idea of not going to sleep. Sleep is what I think about for most of the day.

You really are getting ready to die, aren't you?

We still have little idea why we sleep. Really. But we won't leave the answer there. Instead, let's look at whether we truly *need* to sleep.

Researchers have spent decades attempting to answer this question. First by looking for animals that can get by without sleep, and second by investigating what happens to animals that don't sleep for a while.

The first quest has been a spectacular failure; it seems there are no animals – at least higher animals – that don't sleep. Even *Caenorhabditis elegans*, a worm with just 302 neurons in its brain, goes through periods of quiet inactivity that look sleepish. Going slightly higher up the evolutionary scale, the humble fruit fly makes a good case for the necessity of sleep: without it, they are worse at recalling smells and become sluggish.

We know fruit flies sleep because they can become significantly less responsive to stimuli after we see them remaining still for a few minutes. Researchers have also discovered that their brains' electrical activity changes in these periods. What's more, the kinds of proteins produced by their brain cells also shift during this sleep phase, in a way that mimics what happens in mammalian brains. In other words, we can be fairly sure the flies are sleeping sometimes.

It's harder to catch a dolphin napping. Not because they don't nap, but because they have evolved an extremely clever trick. They sleep with half their brain at a time. This 'unihemispheric' sleep allows the dolphin to maintain awareness of its environment and the dangers it contains. When one side of the brain is sufficiently rested, it wakes up and the other half goes to sleep. It's an evolutionary development that many other marine creatures have also developed and provides a strong suggestion that, while looking out for predators might seem like a high priority, sleep is equally important.

Sometimes, though, dolphins have been seen doing the trick we humans evolved in order to allow ourselves better sleep: they post a guard. Pairs or groups of dolphins that have developed a close bond will trust each other enough to take it in turns to sleep while one (or more) keeps watch.

All of this evidence suggests that sleep, being such a ubiquitous behaviour in nature, must have evolved early in the history of life on Earth. The best guess we have is that it is at least 700 million years old. Why? Because a 700-million-year-old marine worm species called *Platynereis dumerilii* seems to have the raw ingredients of our sleep cycle.

The larva of this ragworm has a primitive eye: a photoreceptor cell that produces an electrical signal in response to light. This is accompanied by a pigment cell. When the photoreceptor detects light, it creates an electrical signal that causes the larva's hairs to move rhythmically, making it swim upward. At the same time, though, the pigment cell produces melatonin and gets darker in the sun, and this partially blocks the light from reaching the photoreceptor. The result is that the larvae rise through the ocean during the day, but the shadow cast by the pigment cell after its long exposure to sunlight eventually stops the electrical signal. The larvae stop swimming and fall back into the darker depths of the ocean until the next day begins. Biologists think this cyclic movement helps protect the larvae from predators and from too much ultraviolet radiation.

Platynereis dumerilii is a weirdly interesting organism. It is, essentially, a 3–4-centimetre-long bag of eggs or sperm, depending on its gender. Put a male and a female together into the same bowl and their pheromones cause a frenzied dance, followed by a release of eggs and sperm. After a short while, the bowl contains a clutch of developing embryos – and two dead adult ragworms. Evolution can be cruel.

The fact that we don't tend to die after sex is a bit of evolutionary good fortune for us, because we seem to be related, with common ancestors. We think this because ragworms contain physiology that looks remarkably like certain structures found in the human brain.

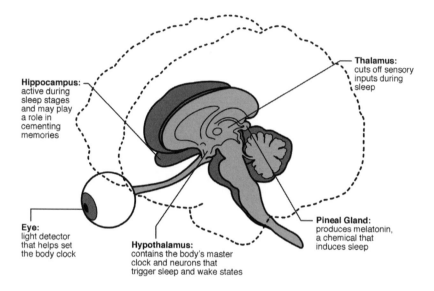

Hippocampus: active during sleep stages and may play a role in cementing memories

Thalamus: cuts off sensory inputs during sleep

Eye: light detector that helps set the body clock

Hypothalamus: contains the body's master clock and neurons that trigger sleep and wake states

Pineal Gland: produces melatonin, a chemical that induces sleep

Various parts of the brain work together to control sleep

The worm brain contains something mirroring our pineal gland, for instance. This is where melatonin, an essential cue to our sleep–wake cycle, is produced. What's more, detective work involving a technique known as 'molecular fingerprinting' has shown a close relationship between the worm's light receptor and the rods and cones that sense light in the retina of the human eye.

This, then, is our best guess as to where sleep began: thanks to evolution's work on some marine worms, mammalian brains produce melatonin when light levels fall, shutting down our wakefulness.

None of this explains precisely what sleep does for us, though. Yes, sleep clearly serves some purpose, because it is ubiquitous. But what happens while we sleep? Why can't Nancy do without it and destroy Freddy's power over her?

What Happens When We Don't Sleep?

This was Johnny Depp's first film. He only went to the auditions to keep his friend Jackie Earle Haley company.

Three first names? Jackie must have got a part.

Nope. But Johnny's face was enough to get him the role of Nancy's boyfriend Glen.

Fair enough. How could you see the young Johnny Depp and not put him in your film? I bet Jackie was pissed off, though.

I'm sure he channelled it into his role as Freddy in the 2010 remake.

I hope he didn't go full method.

Ẁe have already noted that fruit flies are mentally and physically sluggish when sleep-deprived. That doesn't come as a surprise to anyone.* After all, we've all experienced what it's like to be jet-lagged, or just overtired. But just how dangerous that state can be was demonstrated in an experiment on rats in 1983.

Allan Rechtschaffen and his colleagues put two rats on an ingenious but cruel apparatus that consisted of a rotating disc over a tank of water with a barrier separating the two animals. One of the rat's brains was wired to a device that started the disc spinning every time the rat fell asleep. If this poor creature (let's call it Rat A) stayed asleep, the disc would carry it to the barrier, where it would fall into the water. The only way for Rat A to escape an unwanted bath was for it to walk in the opposite direction to the spin. In other words, Rat A could never sleep for more than a moment.

Rat B was having a much better time of it. It could sleep while Rat A was awake and the disc was stationary. And when Rat A fell asleep and the disc began to spin, Rat B could wake up refreshed and enjoy a pleasant stroll against the spin.

The exercise for the rats added up to about a mile's walk every day. Rat A, sleep-deprived and exhausted, died within five days.

In further experiments, different versions of Rat A lived long enough to survive the experiment, but they always showed severe trauma. Their fur became unkempt, they had lesions on their skin, their gait was unstable and their brain signals were measurably diminished. Autopsies on the rats that died were telling: they revealed ulcers, internal

---

* Pigeons seem to function normally when sleep-deprived. This is possibly an indicator of how stupid and sluggish pigeons are *all* the time.

bleeding, collapsed lungs, withered testicles and swollen bladders. The rats that were able to sleep showed no such symptoms.

How often should I sleep?

In 1992 a psychobiologist called Thomas Wehr changed the day/night routine for seven volunteers. Over a four-week period, they lived in accommodation where the light was strictly controlled and the number of daylight hours drastically reduced. Instead of the normal sixteen hours of light, they experienced just ten hours a day. The result? They altered their sleep routine so that it was 'biphasic'. In other words, they divided their shut-eye into two portions.

Split sleep – whether it is split into two phases or many – is not uncommon in the animal kingdom. And it used to be common for humans. Dickens, Chaucer and other writers mention 'first sleep' and 'second sleep'. It seems that before the invention of the electric light, people tended to go to sleep at dusk, and get in a few hours of shut-eye before waking around midnight. They would then perform various tasks – tend fires, do some cooking, have sex maybe – before going back to sleep. Many medical texts from the sixteenth and seventeenth centuries suggest that this was the ideal time to conceive children, mostly because you'd be a bit refreshed and able to make a better fist of it.

These days, though, it's not generally recommended. The twenty-first-century medical advice is to get all your sleep in just one block. This gives your body the best opportunity to carry out all the restorative biochemical processes that sleep makes possible.

We can conclude from this somewhat gruesome experiment that sleep prevents some extremely dangerous problems developing, in rats at the very least. It's also true of mice: experiments that deprived them of sleep suggested that their brains began to actually destroy themselves. We know that from the glial cells. They are part of the support structure for the brain's neurons and normally responsible for jobs such as getting rid of the cellular detritus created in day-to-day life and pruning unwanted connections between neurons. In fact, some sleep researchers are beginning to think that this is the main purpose of sleep: to prune some synaptic networks in the brain and to strengthen others that are useful. This, it seems, is why sleep is useful for consolidating memories. Experiments have shown that animals that have learned a new task will perform it significantly better after a sleep. However, when not regulated by proper sleep, the glial cells seem to go haywire, indiscriminately eating perfectly healthy brain tissue.

While we sleep, the body also releases growth hormones and increases production of some brain proteins. It sinks into a restful, low-energy state like an idling engine. Blood pressure drops. It's definitely good for you, whatever is actually going on. And we can certainly tell that from what happens when we don't sleep.

At some point in our lives, all of us will suffer sleep loss to some extent. It is becoming a huge problem. The WHO recommends we get eight hours of sleep a night, but in the developed world two-thirds of us are failing to heed that recommendation. The consequences of this are startling. Lose just 16 per cent of your required sleep – achieving what seems like a respectable 6.75 hours a night – and only medical intervention will allow you to live past your early sixties. This is a particular problem for men: males who report getting less sleep than they would like suffer a 29 per cent reduction in sperm count. You'll remember from Chapter 5 where that leads.

It's no overstatement to say that many of us unwittingly risk our lives, and the lives of others, because of sleep deprivation. Drive a car after less than five hours' sleep and you are over four times more likely to be involved in a crash. Dial your sleep back to four hours and the likelihood increases to eleven-and-a-half times.

We celebrate those who eschew sleep in order to get things done – British Prime Minister Margaret Thatcher famously got by on four hours a night and once said, 'sleep is for wimps'. She eventually died of a stroke after a bout of dementia, albeit at eighty-eight years old – not bad going, we have to admit. We certainly can't prove there's a link in Thatcher's case, but experiments have shown that there is a strong link between sleep loss and dementia. Interestingly, that link has to do with dreaming, specifically 'rapid eye movement' (REM) sleep – the phase of sleep where we dream. A loss in REM sleep is strongly linked to an increased risk of dementia. Dreaming is important to our brains, it seems. And, of course, the same goes for nightmares.

What, Exactly, Is a Dream?

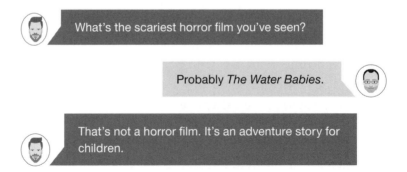

What's the scariest horror film you've seen?

Probably *The Water Babies*.

That's not a horror film. It's an adventure story for children.

Yes, but it stars Billie Whitelaw, the nanny from *The Omen*. I watched *The Omen* when I was eleven and was so freaked out that I can't handle anything she's in.

You really are tragic sometimes.

Don't laugh, it's a genuine phobia. The first time I watched *The Water Babies* with my children I had to leave the room.*

'I dreamed about a guy in a dirty red and green sweater,' Nancy tells Tina at the start of *A Nightmare on Elm Street*. So what does that mean? The short answer is, it's an internal reality. When researchers record the brain activity of a person who is dreaming, it is indistinguishable from someone who is awake. Somehow, though, their brain contrives to paralyze the muscles that would normally be under their conscious control (apart from the eye muscles, which can roll around wildly in their sockets). That is, presumably, so that they can't act on the reality that's playing out in their imagination.

It's a useful mechanism, because it seems we need to dream. Most of the world's languages have a phrase that means, roughly, 'I slept on it.' Dreams appear to be a vital part of decision-making, allowing us to process emotions associated with experiences and dilemmas of the day, and thus deal with them better. University of California sleep researcher Matthew Walker describes dreaming as a session of 'overnight

* True story.

therapy'. That emotional processing also allows us to create neutral memories of events, stripped of the intense emotion and making them more straightforward to recall. In people with post-traumatic stress disorder (PTSD), dreaming has proved extraordinarily useful in helping them cope with triggers that might take them back into a traumatized state.

None of this is settled, however. Some researchers argue that dreams have no significance or purpose: they are just a by-product of all that brain-cleaning the glial cells are doing. Yet another viewpoint says our dreams are an evolutionary strategy that prepares us for action that might save our lives. According to this camp, dreams are so frequently action-packed because they involve rehearsal of the moves that will get us through life-threatening scenarios.

One thing that does seem clear is that dreams play a role in laying down memories, which are stored in the hippocampus – a small, seahorse-shaped structure embedded deep in the base of the brain. When researchers prevented the electromagnetic emissions from the brain associated with REM sleep from reaching the hippocampus of mice, those mice were unable to remember how to perform tasks they had learned during the day. Blocking non-REM brain signals had no effect.

Dreams also make us wiser, Walker reckons. The consolidation of learning is tied together in REM sleep with picking out the salient parts of what has been learned, so that the brain develops a kind of synthesis of the whole experience – wisdom that can be applied elsewhere.

Perhaps the most exciting thing about dreams, though, is that you can learn to control them, and make decisions about how they should play out. It's the kind of skill you need if you're going to stand up to Freddy Krueger.

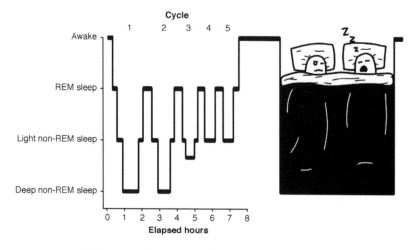

A night's sleep goes through multiple stages

The experience is called lucid dreaming, and some people can do it naturally.* While in the REM phase of their sleep cycle, they retain an awareness that they are dreaming and, often, can take control of the plot. So they might, for instance, meet someone they fancy and get to flirt with them in a conscious, decision-making manner. Or they might just indulge in a few superhuman feats, jumping across canyons and generally acting like a demigod. Lucid dreaming is fun.

If you are among the majority who can't lucid dream naturally, you'll be glad to know you can learn. To train yourself in this art, you have to work on it during the daytime. Remember the spinning top in Christopher Nolan's *Inception*? You need something like that – something that's a trigger to tell your conscious mind that you're dreaming but open to it taking control. Lucid dreaming coach Charlie Morley suggests repeating a simple mantra before you go to sleep: 'Tonight I remember my dreams. I have excellent recall of my dreams.'

* Our copyeditor Julia, for example.

While you were sleeping

You can do astonishing things while you sleep. You can drive a car, for instance, or have sex. You can even kill someone.

That's what happened to British man Brian Thomas. In 2009, he was acquitted of the murder of his wife, whom he had strangled. According to the defence, Thomas had a sleep disorder that rendered him incapable of controlling his actions while in a sleepwalking state.

Few people understand the depth of guilt that Thomas now lives with, but Canadian Kenneth Parks is one. In 1987, Parks killed his mother- and father-in-law during an episode of sleepwalking in which he had driven to his in-laws' house and even armed himself with a knife from their kitchen. Parks too was acquitted because of a lack of culpability for his actions.

Such states can be triggered during the 'slow wave' phase of deep sleep. The sleepers aren't dreaming in this phase, so the muscle paralysis that prevents us from acting out our dreams isn't available to hold them back.

It seems that all of these conditions are triggered by some sort of glitch in the brain as it moves between sleep states. Hearing a doorbell or a dog bark, or sometimes taking certain sleep medication, the brain ends up trapped between deep sleep and wakefulness. We know this because a Swiss researcher once managed to scan a sixteen-year-old's brain while he was sleepwalking – quite a feat. The signals from the boy's brain indicated that he was deep in dreamless sleep, while still registering emotional states.

Once in this in-between state, all bets are off. The sleepwalkers* might perform routine tasks such as getting

---

* Yes, Julia sleepwalks too.

dressed or leaving the house. They have been known to get in the car and go to their office. They might eat; one woman reported gaining 23 kilograms because of sleep-eating. In Australia, a woman woke up with a paintbrush in her hand and found she had painted the front door of her house. In some cases, known as sexsomnia, sleeping people have forced themselves on their partners; sleep sex is not an uncommon occurrence, and can be a traumatic experience for both partners.

You could add in an intense study of your hand, repeated at intervals throughout the day. Then, when you're dreaming, you might dream about studying your hand, see something odd in it – an extra digit, perhaps – and achieve a conscious awareness that you must be dreaming. Once you have that in place, the awareness that you are dreaming will become more and more routine. Then, gradually, you can learn to make a decision that directs your dream-self to act in a certain way, do something interesting or even speak a certain phrase. Some people have even managed to communicate with the outside world – through controlled, pre-agreed eye movements, for example – while still dreaming.

As you get better and better at it, the whole process starts to become as natural as controlling a video game, and that's when you can start to have fun. Some lucid dreamers report being able to fly, have sex or even – as one nineteenth-century lucid dreamer reported – blowing their own brains out.

That intrepid individual was Marie-Jean-Léon Lecoq, also known as the French aristocrat the Marquis d'Hervey de Saint Denys. This pioneer of lucid dreaming research recorded hundreds of nights of dream activity. He could make himself wander through landscapes he had visited by day, or engage in chivalrous – and not so chivalrous – behaviour. The marquis became so good at controlling his dreams that he could use a sheer effort of will to imagine weapons into his hands so that he was equipped with whatever he needed for an adventure. Eventually, he wrote his experiences up in a book called *Dreams and How to Guide Them*.

Astonishingly, the marquis records having a *Nightmare on Elm Street* experience: he was chased by a monster through a maze of rooms. In the end, he used his willpower to turn around and stare down the monster, which caused the beast to fade away. So it seems entirely plausible that (spoiler alert) Nancy is able to disable Freddy by declaring that she's no longer afraid of him.

For all the fun that the marquis had, one group of people who are particularly prone to lucid dreaming take no pleasure in it whatsoever. For the poor souls who suffer from narcolepsy, our movie's tagline – whatever you do, don't fall asleep – must be particularly haunting.

Can Sleep Problems Be Fatal?

> Which of us would die first in a stereotypical horror movie?

> Well I'm the good-looking hero type, so I don't think I'm lasting terribly long.

> What about the science-loving nerd? Do nerds get spared?

They don't even get into the movie.

Because they're too sensible and analytical and horror films are all about emotion?

No, because horror films are all about people who have real-life friends.

Narcolepsy is often portrayed as comic. After all, what could be more humorous than someone who spontaneously exits the conscious world and falls asleep against their will? Well, everything, it turns out. Narcolepsy is a living nightmare.

Around 1 in 2500 people suffer from narcolepsy. It's not just about falling asleep; it brings on a range of conditions. There's cataplexy, where an emotion as mundane as mirth or anger cuts all muscle activity for a few seconds – or a few minutes if you're particularly unlucky. It makes it look like you've fallen asleep when you haven't – you're fully conscious, and probably embarrassed if not terrified. Sometimes even an orgasm can trigger a bout of cataplexy. There are excessive and super-vivid bouts of dreaming, which fracture night-time sleep so much that it causes a perverse kind of insomnia. There is a drop in metabolism, resulting in dramatic weight gain.

It's not yet clear why some unfortunate people are narcoleptic, but there seem to be a range of factors that have to come together in a particularly brutal alignment. The first is a genetic issue: inheriting a particular version of a gene known as HLA-DQB1*0602, which helps the immune system make decisions about what it should attack in the body. Around 25 per cent of Europeans have this genetic variant, but it is found in 98 per cent of narcoleptics.

The next element of the perfect storm seems to be a close encounter with a virus or bacterium that stresses the immune system in a way that makes it overreact. Put simply, the wrong pathogen can cause the immune system to attack the brain and wipe out 30,000 of the neurons in the hypothalamus. This is a serious matter. These neurons are the only ones that produce chemicals called orexin (or hypocretin). These chemicals regulate the body's wakefulness. Without orexin, you're effectively doomed to becoming narcoleptic. The suggestion that you don't fall asleep is entirely pointless: it's utterly beyond your control.

As if things weren't bad enough for narcoleptics, they are also more likely than others to suffer sleep paralysis, where the brain wakes up only to find that the body is stuck in a REM-paralysis. This is often accompanied by the hallucinations that occur in the twilight zone between waking and sleep – sometimes known as 'night terrors'. Sufferers all describe the same sense of a malevolent presence or being physically assaulted – a huge weight pressing down on their chest, or being pulled, or choked, or smothered and dragged into hell. Some say they levitate above the bed or see a dark, twisted figure that is bent on doing them harm. Some smell a stench of sulphur. In all cases they are paralyzed, unable to help themselves, unable to cry out for help from others, unable to express the sheer physical terror they are experiencing.

Such experiences are common to almost every culture in the world. In Newfoundland they call it the 'Old Hag'. In

Hong Kong, it's the 'ghost oppression'. The inhabitants of St Lucia call it 'kokma'. Here's one account, cited by Julia Santomauro and Christopher C. French in *The Psychologist*:

> I'm lying on my back with my eyes closed and I feel a crushing weight on my chest. I've felt this before, so I'm not scared. I open my eyes just a little bit and I see this two-dimensional grey humanoid on top of me with three-dimensional dirty grey hair hanging in my face. He is clutching my chest and dragging me down the bed into a wooden box that looks like a casket at the foot of my bed. I know that if he drags me into the box that I will die. I turn my head sideways and look into the mirror that faces my bed and watch myself being pulled down the bed towards the box. I am absolutely terrified by this point and I finally wake up, when I am transported back to the top of my bed with my head looking up at the ceiling.

It seems that, in extreme circumstances, such night-time terrors do have the power to kill. The inspiration for *A Nightmare on Elm Street* came when Wes Craven read a newspaper article that chronicled a tragic story of a family who had come to the US after escaping the Cambodian Killing Fields. The youngest member of the family had such disturbing nightmares of being hunted after the trauma in Cambodia that he tried to avoid going to sleep. Sometimes he would avoid sleep for days at a time, but one day he fell asleep after a bout of sleep deprivation and never woke up. His parents heard him screaming in the middle of the night and rushed to his side to find him dead.

His is not the only such case. For a few years in the late 1970s and early 1980s, US doctors registered hundreds of deaths of Asian men as 'sudden unexpected nocturnal death syndrome'. They were often reported as dying with a terrified expression on their faces.

It took a while to make sense of what some termed a kind of 'voodoo death'. But it turned out that most of the men had come to the US after traumatic experiences in Cambodia and Vietnam, and were terrified by their dreams. Families reported these men sometimes setting alarm clocks to go off every half hour so that they wouldn't start to dream. Doctors eventually identified them as also having 'Brugada syndrome', a heart abnormality relatively common in men from Southeast Asia. Brugada syndrome gives rise to an erratic pulse and that, combined with sleep deprivation, seemed to be enough to trigger a fatal cardiac arrest.

For all the horror of narcolepsy and sleep paralysis, it's unlikely to kill anyone without a pre-existing medical problem – even when night terrors set in. But the stress of staying permanently awake probably would. We know this not because of those sleep-deprived rats on the turntable, but because it regularly happens to one unfortunate set of people.

This is a true horror story. There are twenty-six families in the world where a genetic aberration causes an inability to sleep. It usually first manifests as a sudden mild insomnia that gets worse over a matter of months. When a sufferer does manage to get to sleep, dreams can be wild and vivid. Next there is a physical and mental deterioration. There is weight loss, forgetfulness, confusion, double vision, rapid, uncontrollable eye movements, muscle spasms... and then – understandably – paranoia and panic attacks. It is almost as if the body itself starts to panic. Men suffer erectile dysfunction; women are plunged into menopause. There can be uncontrollable crying, anxiety, depression and – eventually – dementia.

This is the final act of 'fatal familial insomnia': a descent into the appalling disconnection from the outside world as the brain shuts itself down for good. There is no cure. There are no ongoing drug trials or useful therapies. If you are unlucky enough to be one of the few dozen people in the world who has ever been diagnosed with fatal familial insomnia, medicine can do nothing for you.

See also

There's no shortage of movies about sleep and dreaming. Christopher Nolan has had a go at both. In Nolan's *Insomnia*, Al Pacino plays a sleep-deprived detective investigating a murder in Alaska. In *Inception*, Leonardo DiCaprio is invading and manipulating dreams. Both are definitely worth your time, as is *Vanilla Sky*, where Tom Cruise plays (slight spoiler alert) a man whose lucid dreams are part of a long-term medical issue. Then there's *The Machinist*, where Christian Bale plays an emaciated insomniac who begins to suffer paranoid delusions. It's alarming on many levels, but will reassure you that Bale will have had no trouble losing the 18 kilograms he gained to play Dick Cheney in *Vice*: he lost 28 kilograms for this role.

Less alarming is *The Science of Sleep*, the initial story of which was written by a ten-year-old. You won't be surprised to learn that it's not really about the science of sleep. Instead, it's a surrealist French romcom – and, as you'd expect from Michel Gondry, the director of *Eternal Sunshine of the Spotless Mind*, it's really good. *While You Were Sleeping* is actually about a man in a coma; don't be fooled. And the less said about *The Adventures of Sharkboy and Lavagirl* the better.

Having laid out the worst that can happen – and maybe given you nightmares – perhaps we should make amends with a few scientific tips for getting a good night's rest. The first science-inspired innovation is clear: get science-inspired technology out of your bedroom. That's because our phones, tablets and computers emit a blue light that sends completely the wrong signal: it shouts 'wake up, it's daytime' at our brains. The blue light from LEDs is a stimulant; the last thing we need last thing at night.

That said, we are learning how to benefit from technology such as sleep trackers. By monitoring our heart rate, temperature, movements and breathing, these sensors can map exactly where we are in the sleep cycle, and wake us at a point where we are most able to surface without feeling groggy. That's why companies such as Apple are looking into things like the iSheet: bed linen with embedded sensors that will help improve the quality of sleep. They could even send information to our employers, who might reward good sleep habits because of the extra productivity and fewer sick days they engender.*

Essentially, though, expert advice is fairly straightforward. Dim the lights in your house a couple of hours before bedtime. Keep the bedroom cool, because your core temperature needs to drop for you to sleep well. And, whatever you do, do not watch *A Nightmare on Elm Street* just before you turn out the light.

---

* This seems to us like a proper nightmare. But then neither of us actually has a proper job.

8

Hollywood Wants to Kill You... WITH PLANTS!

'MOST PLANTS THRIVE ON ANIMAL WASTE, BUT I'M

AFRAID THIS MUTATION POSSESSES AN APPETITE

FOR THE ANIMAL ITSELF.'

— *The Day of the Triffids* (1962)

I n John Wyndham's *The Day of The Triffids*, towering, venomous plants with a taste for flesh stalk around the world in packs, taking advantage of a handy meteor shower that has blinded all but a handful of humans. The movie poster for the 1962 film exclaims: 'BEWARE THE TRIFFIDS...

they grow... know... walk... talk... stalk... and KILL!' This all seems quite jolly, because we think that we have nothing to fear from plants. Yes, they grow, but they only do that very slowly. As for knowing and walking and talking and stalking – absolutely not! Or so we thought...

Have We Underestimated Plants?

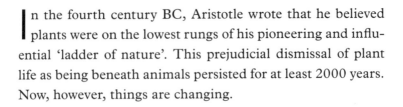

According to *The Sunday Times*, John Wyndham's original story is 'one of those books that haunts you for the rest of your life'.

This is so true. It gave me nightmares for weeks when I read it as a pre-teen.

Even though you could have just run away from them? Wyndham says watching triffids move is like 'watching a man on crutches'.

I know. And they don't like hard surfaces like tarmac or pavements. So in theory you only have to live across the road from them, and you're safe. But I still made my mum get rid of all our houseplants.

In the fourth century BC, Aristotle wrote that he believed plants were on the lowest rungs of his pioneering and influential 'ladder of nature'. This prejudicial dismissal of plant life as being beneath animals persisted for at least 2000 years. Now, however, things are changing.

We can't claim that this was because of the movie. Yes, it is a 'classic' in the sense that it feels familiar, but it is not terribly good. Even the producers knew this: when they finished filming they only had fifty-seven minutes of useable footage. That entire narrative arc in the lighthouse was shamelessly added to pad the movie out to an acceptable length. But anyway, despite their appalling acting skills, plants are definitely on the up.

Traditionally, we have ranked living things primarily by intelligence, focusing the search for smarts on two things: neurons and nervous systems, and directed, controlled movements in response to stimuli. These, we tend to think, are the only source of 'intelligent behaviour'. But, ironically, our thinking about intelligence is probably all wrong.

Let's take brains first. Our bias towards brains is especially clear when you consider that we are tempted to recognize intelligence in a computer – something which we know not to be living – but not in plants. We humans are self-absorbed and, perhaps unavoidably, have a very anthropocentric view of what intelligence must be. So when we look at a computer with its information processing in a central unit, which we have, of course, loosely modelled on our brain, we find it compelling. Does that mean that computers are smarter than plants? No, it does not.

The reason that we have failed for so long to ask questions about plant awareness or intelligence (or even consciousness) is that we just haven't considered those questions worthwhile. That 'we' doesn't include Charles Darwin. Ever the free-thinking legend, Darwin saw things differently. In the nineteenth century he recognized that plants had something about them. He even hypothesized that they might have a kind of 'root brain'. In the early 1900s an Indian biophysicist called Jagdish Chandra Bose picked up on this and started to perform experiments which appeared to corroborate some of Darwin's ideas. He became persuaded that plants do have a form of nervous system, and that this was allowing them to actively monitor and explore their surroundings. But the notion that plants aren't merely a static, unresponsive feedstock for the rest of nature just didn't take hold. Things got worse for plant PR in the 1970s, when a book called *The Secret Life of Plants* was published. On the one hand, this book was extremely popular. But on the other, it was also nonsense. Its hippy-tinged pages spoke of plants exhibiting telepathy and emotion, and enjoying listening to a spot of Wagner. Almost everything in it has been debunked – and done lasting damage to the perception of plant sciences. Now, however, things are finally changing, because a daring group of researchers are facing down the anti-plant bigots.

This new dawn began in 2005, when a small group of scientists set up something they called the Society for Plant Neurobiology. Naturally, their fellow biologists were falling over themselves to criticize, mostly because plants don't have neurons in their biology. One choice reaction from Clifford Slayman, a Yale professor of cellular and molecular physiology, was that this represented the 'last confrontation between the scientific community and the nuthouse'. But the group pressed on, and set themselves to investigate an alternative form of intelligence, one that doesn't require neurons.

While we feel very comfortable discussing intelligence, and relative intelligence, and the kind of things we expect it to allow an organism to do, there is no consensus on what intelligence actually is. So perhaps we should be willing to ascribe intelligence to any organism that successfully performs the task of collecting, storing and using information about its environment to ensure survival. In which case, plants fit the bill.

That's why the plant neurobiology researchers suggested that a plant's behaviour results from gathering and using data from its surroundings and then making a coordinated response, one that is not just a biochemical reflex or programmed into the plant's genetics. The molecular biologist Anthony Trewavas, who himself has made some significant contributions to the field, speaks of plants' 'mindless mastery' – and he means mindless in a good way: who needs a brain?

If you're having trouble seeing how this could work, consider an ant colony. Each ant represents a simple unit that acts according to some fairly simple rules. Look at the colony as a whole though, and these simple units and rules give rise to some complex – apparently intelligent – behaviours. This is known as 'distributed intelligence'. The whole is greater than the sum of its basic parts. It's not dissimilar to the very simple algorithms that give rise to complex swarming behaviour in flocks of birds (just follow the closest bird in your field of vision). Stefano Mancuso, one of the people who set up the Society for Plant Neurobiology (which has, incidentally, since changed its name to the less contentious Society of Plant Signaling and Behavior), believes something similar might be happening with plants.

Specifically, he is building on Darwin's idea of the root brain. Mancuso and his colleagues have identified a section of the root, near the tip, known as the transition zone. For many years the function of this section has been unknown – but there is a lot of electrical activity there, a high concentration of oxygen and a hormone called auxin which is transported in little containers called vesicles. You'll find things with these properties in animals: we call them – you guessed it – neurons.

It's possible, then, that each root tip, a fairly rudimentary structure, is forming part of a larger network and giving rise to a greater, distributed intelligence. That's not all that different to a brain. After all, there is no part of your brain that's the specific 'smart control centre'. It's just a load of neurons – eighty-six billion of them in your case – all working together. No individual one of them is 'clever', but the result is (hopefully) intelligent.

On the move

It's fair to say that plants don't really move across a landscape. There is a tree in Ecuador called the walking palm tree, but it can't actually walk. What happens is that it sends out roots looking for more fertile soil and, when these prove fruitful, the trunk bends towards that location. The old roots then lift into the air and become useless. Relocation to a more fertile location a few metres away can take a couple of years. It's not chasing anyone down the street.

Tumbleweed is a bit more mobile and dangerous – even though it is, strictly speaking, dead. Tumbleweed breaks off from its roots and rolls through a landscape to disperse the seeds within its structure. It is only dangerous because in extreme heat and drought it can burst into flames, helping spread wildfires. Again, it's no triffid.

What's more, not everything involved in operating a higher-level creature has to involve awareness. We tend to forget that we actually *need* some of our nervous system to run without conscious control from the brain. That's why we have an autonomic nervous system that looks after a whole array of processes – breathing and digestion, for example – with very little interference from 'up on high'. Imagine if you had to actually think in order to digest, breathe or have your heart beat faster when you exercise.

The final thing to think about is that having a brain would be a clear disadvantage for a plant. Plants are essentially immobile and therefore extremely vulnerable to attack. In fact, part of their evolutionary strategy is to get eaten. Plants can survive with 90 per cent of their bodies removed – in the film, you can blow holes in a triffid with a shotgun and it doesn't die. Imagine if they had a brain: then they could not survive their grey matter getting eaten or blown away.* It would be a disadvantage; whereas their modular design perfectly suits their largely sessile lifestyle.

In short, as we consider plants, we need to check our prejudice. We're not better, just different. Plants and animals branched off from each other on the evolutionary tree around one-and-a-half billion years ago. Their common ancestor was a unicellular organism, neither plant nor animal. Plants and animals share much of the same genetic code and are far more closely related to each other than either are to bacteria. In fact, our cells are remarkably similar to plant cells – the key differences we learn about at school, like plant cell walls and chloroplasts for photosynthesis, are actually quite superficial. Perhaps the main difference is that animals evolved nervous systems and brains, and plants apparently did not. But that doesn't mean they don't have intelligence.

Nor does it mean that we shouldn't be afraid of them.

---

* Shout out to the planarian flatworm (see Chapter 9) which would laugh in the face of getting its brain blown out.

Should We Fear the Flora?

Scientists are pretty sure that every living thing on Earth has a common ancestor – LUCA.

How do they know it was Italian?

It stands for 'last universal common ancestor' and lived around three-and-a-half billion years ago. Staggering really. We're related, however distantly, to every form of life, whether a fungus, an amoeba or a slime mould.

Ah, slime moulds. They're the pulsating blobs motivated entirely by food? Yes, I can believe that you're related to them.

'Keep behind me,' Tom tells Karen as they escape from the lighthouse. 'There's no sense in getting killed by a plant.' Never a truer word was spoken. As we've seen, plants – even triffids – are largely avoidable. Nonetheless, the chances are that you already have a healthy fear of plants, even if you have watched this movie. You don't go tramping through stinging nettles in shorts or stop to lick a deadly nightshade flower, do you?

Plants enjoy extremely extensive chemical resources, including a whole host of defensive toxins. These are designed to ward off insects and other small herbivores, but some of these toxins can still be lethal to bigger animals like us. Take the *Manchineel* which is found in the Americas. It richly deserves the title of World's Most Dangerous Tree. Locals often mark its bark with a painted red cross to warn people away. Its sap contains a nasty irritant called phorbol, which can cause a horrific rash in humans. A single drop can make the skin blister. Burning the trees releases a smoke that can temporarily blind you and impede your breathing. None of that will kill you, but don't worry, it's got more in its arsenal – specifically, its little round fruit. Eat that and you're a goner.

Then there's the castor plant. It is often grown as an ornamental because it looks nice, and its oil is widely used in food production. But don't mess with its beans. They contain ricin, one of the most lethal naturally occurring poisons. Ricin prevents the body from manufacturing the proteins necessary for its day-to-day biological functions, and eventually causes you to shut down. So if just a little ricin gets into your system, either by injection or ingestion, it will slowly kill you, as Bulgarian defector Georgi Markov found out in 1978. He was walking across London's Waterloo Bridge one morning when agents from his home country assassinated him with a specially-engineered umbrella. The umbrella's tip contained a pneumatic mechanism that injected a ricin-laden pellet into Markov's leg. He developed a fever that evening and four days later he was dead.

Or there are the various types of aconite flower, known as wolfsbane, devil's helmet or monkshood. These have long been used as deadly toxins by hunters looking to kill prey as big as bears or even whales. One single aconite-tipped harpoon is enough to paralyze a whale, so humans who come into contact with even relatively small doses of the poison stand little chance of surviving. Be warned if you're a forager: it looks a bit like wild parsley, but just 5 millilitres

– a teaspoon – of sap from the plant will kill an adult human. In case you were wondering, the International Programme on Chemical Safety (IPCS) reports that, 'No antidote is available.'

It's worth pointing out that plant poisons aren't always a bad thing. Your parents might never have actually said, 'Eat up your vegetables, you need the toxins,' but they should have: that's exactly what vitamins are. We need them because our biology has co-opted plant defence mechanisms as essential weapons in the fight against bacteria, viruses and other disruptors of our normal, healthy biochemistry.

Ultimately, it's about getting the dose right. Just eating the seeds of the *Strychnos nux-vomica* tree, found in Southeast Asia, won't kill you. In fact, some people use them as a treatment for certain conditions (though it has never been scientifically proven that they help). But if you isolate and concentrate the compound involved, you can use it to induce a horrid death that we know as strychnine poisoning. It's what we use to eradicate vermin such as rodents.

So far we've looked at passive defence mechanisms. But in *The Day of the Triffids*, the plants go on the offensive. Does that happen? You bet.

Generally speaking, plants don't need all that many nutrients to survive. Usually, the required rootful of nitrogen, phosphorous and a few other bits and pieces can be drawn up from the soil. But when they live somewhere where those nutrients aren't available, they turn to other food sources.

Take the parasitic dodder vine, for example. This creepy creeper sniffs out its victims. The dodder has virtually no chlorophyll, so it obtains its energy by 'biting' into its victim's vascular system and sucking out the sugary sap from its veins. Time-lapse video of the vine's tendrils look eerily like a snake searching for something. And it is: when researchers investigating its powers hid some potential host plants around a corner, the dodder found them. Not only that, it seemingly made choices, preferring healthy, succulent plants. It's presumed that it is locating these host plants, and selecting the best ones, by 'smelling' the various chemicals those plants are naturally emitting and then growing in that direction. It's hunting, in other words.

Sometimes, plants prefer flesh to flowers. There are around 750 carnivorous species of plant, and they have evolved multiple times, with a wide variety of hunting strategies. The aquatic plant known as the common bladderwort, for instance, has empty chambers called bladders. When a tiny creature – could be a nematode, a water flea, even a tadpole – ambles past, it disturbs trigger hairs, which open the chamber. Water rushes into the chamber, effectively sucking the unwitting animal in. This happens extremely quickly, giving the animal no time to take evasive action. Within one-thousandth of a second the unlucky creature is trapped in the chamber. Then the bladderwort starts to release its digestive enzymes. Once the animal has been broken down, the plant squeezes the water and any indigestible remains back out, and gets ready for another delicious meal.

Pitcher plants also use a chamber for catching animals. A variety called *Nepenthes rajah* found in the tropics of Borneo has bucket-like pitchers which can grow up to 16 inches long, and hold up to 2.5 litres of water. Insects wander in looking for food and then can't clamber back out, either because the interior is waxy and slippery, or because of an array of downward pointing spikes around the rim. Once it senses its prey has fallen in, the pitcher plant secretes digestive enzymes into the water and it is game over for the insect. Bigger animals can fall prey to the pitcher plant too – these units can digest lizards, small bats and even rodents.

Then there is the most iconic of the carnivorous plants – the Venus flytrap. Its snapping jaws are the most reminiscent of an animal predator, and as such we tend to find them both fascinating and sinister – especially since we learned that they do some rudimentary counting in order to catch their prey without wasting too much energy.

Venus flytrap leaves emit a sweet smell to attract insects. When an insect lands on the leaf, it will brush against one of the trigger hairs. This sends an electrical impulse through the leaves. But one trigger isn't enough to initiate closure. The plant does not want to expend valuable energy on responding to a false positive – there's no point wasting resources on trying to trap a prey that has already escaped. And so it waits for a second hair to be disturbed.

If that happens within about twenty seconds of the first trigger, the leaves snap shut. This happens because the second electrical impulse opens some of the plant's pores, allowing water to move through the plant and creating a pressure change which causes the leaves to close. It's a hydraulic mechanism operated by an electrical switch linked to a pressure sensor. This is a clear example of a plant processing and responding to information, in real time and in deadly fashion.

You won't be surprised to hear that, once the insect is trapped, the Venus flytrap starts to release its digestive enzymes. But it also continues to register the number of hair brushes. The more brushes, the bigger the insect, and it will release more enzymes accordingly. This is sophisticated, efficient stuff.

And while we're on the subject of sophisticated, let's talk about plants talking.

Can Plants Communicate?

> I just found out that there's a 2001 sequel to Wyndham's book. In it, some of the population of the Isle of Wight develop immunity to triffid venom and can return to the mainland.

> That's because Wyndham's original book doesn't resolve the triffid threat: the main character goes to the Isle of Wight to try to figure out what to do.

> I've been to the Isle of Wight. I think I'd rather face the triffids.

> Well, you've clearly never been on the toboggan run at Robin Hill Country Park. It's world class.

Plants have a bizarrely well-developed social life. Down in the soil, the ecosystem around roots is teeming with communication and cooperation. Fungi and bacteria have a symbiotic relationship with the roots – they help the roots absorb water and nutrients, and in return get a steady stream of nutrients for themselves. Everyone's a winner. Not only that though: in what one academic paper pleasingly dubbed the 'wood wide web', fungal threads between tree populations – even between different species – can form a single network.

It's a supportive, collaborative system. Water and nutrients travel from trees with surplus food to ones that are hungry. For example, larger trees help out seedlings until they've grown sufficiently tall to reach the light. There is even mutually beneficial trading between species across the year, so an evergreen will provide a deciduous tree with some sugars in the winter and then 'call in the debt' in the summer. Older trees seem to be super-connected hubs, offering large numbers of connections. The entire forest appears to function better due to this invisible cooperation.

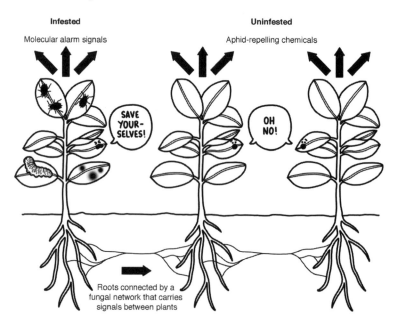

Plants attacked by pests will alert other plants to the danger of infestation

Plants can also use this underground web to signal to one another. If you subject a row of plants to drought conditions, a message can travel to plants that are five rows away but connected to the water-starved part of the population by their roots. These distant plants then prepare for a lack of water by closing the stomata in their leaves and preventing moisture escape. Plants just as close to the original row, but not connected by the roots, show no such response. They do not get the memo.

It's not just one big love-in with plants, though. In some instances, they will work with other members of the same species at the expense of others. The response of knotweeds to an attack by insects or animals depends on the identity of their close neighbours. If they are with other knotweeds, they focus on defence, by flooding their leaves with toxins. But if they're surrounded by bunch grass, they forgo defence in favour of aggressive growth. Effectively, they are relying on the bunch grass to take care of defence. It's a clever strategy, and is one potential explanation of knotweed's runaway success as an invasive species.

The knotweed's tactic is a bit underhand, but some plants are out-and-out aggressors. The common reed, currently taking over the marshy wetlands of North America, poisons its competitors by secreting an acid from its roots. Very naughty. This is actually an extreme version of something that many plants do: it's known as allelopathy, which means the production of chemicals to inhibit the growth of competitors. Generally, that just means encouraging other plants to keep their distance, but this reed's acid is so toxic it dissolves the structural proteins in the roots of its unrelated neighbours, silently killing them.

Plants can also recognize relatives, although how they do so is, again, a bit of a mystery. In evolutionary terms, there are clear advantages to helping out relations (ultimately every living thing wants its genes to be passed on to future generations) and these 'kin-specific' behaviours are also seen throughout the animal kingdom. Psychologists have shown that even humans are subject to this: you are more likely to help a blood relative than a stranger. In the last few decades scientists have started to see plants doing the same thing. Some restrict their root growth or alter the number of flowers they produce to give space to related plants. Others shift their leaf positions to limit shading of familial neighbours.

We started to really appreciate this in 2007, when Canadian biologist Susan Dudley performed an extraordinary experiment with North American sea rocket, a small shrub that tends to grow on beaches and dunes. She grew some in pots with relatives, and others in pots with unrelated plants of the same species. The ones grown with 'strangers' grew extensive root systems, competing keenly for nutrients and water. But the ones grown with family restricted their root growth, presumably to allow their kin to flourish. Subsequent research suggests that the signals which indicate kinship are contained within exudates, a heady mix of soluble compounds which are secreted by the roots into the soil. How these exudates provide the information about relatedness remains unknown.

And this is not just going on beneath the ground. Plants also signal to one another using an extensive vocabulary of volatile, airborne chemicals. Experiments with sagebrush have shown that if you simulate insect munching by clipping an individual plant's leaves early in the season, the clipped plant and its neighbours will suffer much less damage for the rest of the season. It seems that the attacked plant is releasing chemicals which are picked up by nearby plants – alerting them to prepare for more attacks.* This effect appears to be more pronounced with closely related plants, again suggesting some kin recognition is at work.

* Nowhere in the scientific literature is this being called 'leavesdropping', which is inexcusable. We are currently campaigning for the term's introduction.

Antelope versus acacia

One of the most surprising botanical discoveries came in 1983, when it became clear that acacia trees in the African savannah were banding together in a self-defence campaign. Normally the trees produce only a small amount of a compound called tannin, which makes the leaves bitter and unpleasant to the taste. When its leaves are damaged – by a hungry kudu antelope, for example – an acacia produces much more tannin as a form of self-defence. But it also releases a compound called ethylene into the air. Nearby trees sense this chemical and increase their tannin production as a means of self-defence. And in extreme conditions, such as drought, when a kudu's appetite could kill a water-starved tree, they manufacture so much tannin that it stops the kudu's liver from functioning. In South African game ranches, where the kudu are fenced in and have no choice but to try to eat the acacia, this resulted in the deaths of hundreds of kudu through the dry season.

It's not all about chemicals: there is some evidence that plants use sound to communicate. Young corn plant roots, when grown in water, emit little clicks. And if those clicks are recorded and played back to them, the roots change their growth behaviour – the roots, it seems, are chatting.

How is this possible? Well, your ears contain tiny hairs that bend when hit by the vibrating air of a sound wave. The bent hairs create an electrical signal that the brain interprets as sound. Plants have a similar system: the cell membranes contain a type of protein that deforms when subjected to sound waves. The deformation allows ions to cross the membrane, creating a charge difference between the inside and outside of the cell, which in turn generates an electrical current.

Plants don't have a brain in which these signals are experienced as sounds, but they do have sensors that allow the plant to respond in the appropriate way. Researchers have recently shown, for instance, that when the evening primrose flower hears bees buzzing, it starts to produce nectar which is up to 20 per cent sweeter. The flower is enticing the bees over with its sugary goodies. Quite how the flowers are detecting the buzzing is unclear, but one idea is that the buzzing causes the flowers to vibrate, and that its petals act a bit like ears – receiving and amplifying the sounds.

On a slightly less pleasant note, if you broadcast the sound of a munching caterpillar near a plant, it will take action to defend itself. The leaves become flooded with toxins or alter their texture in order to become less digestible. In the case of corn and some bean plants, the noise of an approaching caterpillar makes the leaves release a volatile chemical that summons parasitic wasps. These wasps follow the scent and attack the caterpillars – effectively, the plant has called in the cavalry.

So far we've learned about plants communicating, discerning friend from foe and going on the attack. Perhaps the weirdest thing is yet to come: it's not just us humans that can be taught stuff – plants learn too.

Can You Teach An Old Plant New Tricks?

> If nothing else, this must be giving vegans something to think about.

> Not just vegans. We should all be giving our leafy brethren much more respect.

> Would you say you're more obsessed with the octopus or plants these days?

> That's an impossible question. Like asking me to choose my favourite child.

> Conjures up a delightful image of an Edwards family portrait.

In *The Day of the Triffids*, the plants don't come across as particularly intelligent. When they surround the house in Spain, they're redolent of a zombie horde. It's far more *Dawn of the Dead* than, say, *Alien*. But some plants are intelligent enough to learn, as evolutionary biologist Professor Monica Gagliano will tell you.

Gagliano has spent a great deal of time trying to figure out just what plants are capable of. The most impressive thing, she decided, would be if plants can adapt their behaviour based on their experience of the environment – learn, in other words. But how do you teach something to a plant?

The first step is to test for the most basic level of learning: habituation. We habituate all the time, which is to say, we ignore stuff in our environment that is irrelevant to our needs or our safety. To pay attention to things that have no impact on us is to waste valuable resources.

Gagliano began her test for habituation by dropping a mimosa plant on to the ground. This, she reasoned, is not something that the plants would have experienced in their evolutionary history: it's a novel experience, and the plant's reaction would be a good test of its ability to learn.

It is well-known that when you touch a mimosa, or disturb it in some way, it closes its leaves. This is a defence mechanism that probably evolved to scare insects away. Gagliano started by dropping her mimosas from just 15 centimetres above the ground, and at first the plants responded as she expected – they closed their leaves. But after the fourth, fifth or sixth drop, they stopped responding. The leaves stayed open.

They weren't just fatigued from all the leaf exertions. The plants continued to respond to physical touch – a possible insect attack – by closing their leaves. Instead, it seems that the mimosas had decided that this new falling experience was not actually dangerous and closing up the leaves was just a waste of energy. This is exactly the kind of habituation you find in animals. The plants had learned from experience.

It gets weirder. When Gagliano repeated the drops a week later, the plants remembered. Once again, they didn't react. So they not only learned something; they also stored the information they had learned. Even a month later, the plants still remembered not to bother closing their leaves if they felt a sudden fall. This is clear evidence of some sort of long-term memory. And it stacks up pretty well against the habituation of small animals – bees, for example, tend to remember their habituation for just forty-eight hours.

Impressed? You should be. But there's more. Gagliano next decided to test whether plants were capable of associative learning. This is the type of learning made most famous by Pavlov and his hungry dogs, where a training regime of being fed after a bell rings eventually caused dogs to salivate uncontrollably at the mere sound of a bell.

This time, Gagliano took pea plants and set up something

called a 'Y-maze'. It's not the trickiest maze in the world: the pea plant has just two options – grow up the left-hand tube or the right-hand tube.

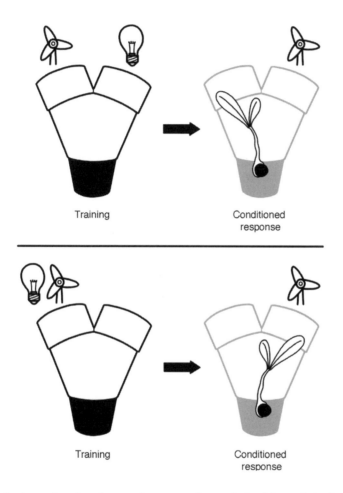

A plant that has learned to associate wind with no light (top) will grow away from the wind. A plant that has learned wind and light come together (bottom) will grow towards the wind, even in the absence of light

The experiment uses two growth stimuli: light and wind. Gagliano started by shining light down the left side, and incorporated a fan that blew air down the same side. You won't be surprised to hear that the pea plants grew off to the left in these conditions, because the light is their food source.

But then Gagliano switched things up. Now there was no light; she just blew the fan down the right-hand side. And 62 per cent of the pea plants grew towards the right, presumably because they had learned to associate the wind with the light.

It was a startling enough result to convince even sceptical biologists that plants could learn. When Gagliano had tried to get her paper about dropping mimosas published, she had been turned down by ten separate journals. The new work with the pea plants went straight into *Nature*, one of the most prestigious scientific journals in the world.

It turns out that pea plants aren't just associative learners: they're gamblers too. You can show this by growing the plants in a 'split pot', where they can choose to grow into one of two different soils. The experimenter can control the soil's nutrient levels and, if the available nutrition is adequate, the plants will favour soil which has an unchanging concentration of nutrients. This is risk-averse behaviour; playing it safe, effectively. But if nutrient levels in both soils are low, they will favour a soil where the nutrient level varies over time. It's a risky strategy, but when desperate a varying nutrient level might just provide enough for survival.

It feels like we've already proved that plants are – in their own way – intelligent and sentient. But we're going to push our luck now and tell you that they can even do simple arithmetic. That's right. Plants are out there doing maths.

During the day, plants get energy from sunlight, but

that energy source isn't available at night. That's a problem because the basic cellular processes still need energy. By now it won't come as any surprise to you to learn that plants are clever enough to store some of the energy they produce in the daytime in the form of starch. When night falls, they break down the starch at a constant rate and release the energy.

What's really interesting, though, is that by the time dawn comes they have pretty much used up the stored starch and are ready to start over again. This implies that they are budgeting correctly – they know how much starch they have, and how much time they have to ration it for so that they only run out at dawn. Researchers looking into this have controlled the lighting in their labs so that they effectively change the length of the plant's night. And what happens? You guessed it. The plants seamlessly recalculate, adjust their starch degradation rate and still run out of their food reserves at the cusp of expected dawn.

The only way they can do this is if they first have an awareness of time – plants, like animals, have an internal circadian clock – and second if they can perform a calculation that involves division. Basically, they have to divide the amount of starch by the expected length of time until dawn.

How does a plant do this? We're not sure, but one explanation is that there are two particular protein molecules involved. One is associated with the quantity of starch and the other with the time until dawn. The first molecule increases the rate of starch breakdown, while the second inhibits the rate of starch breakdown. So they act in opposition. And the plant controls the relative amounts of the two molecules in its system to control the rate of starch use. Pretty clever stuff.

See also

The 1986 remake of the classic B-movie *Little Shop of Horrors* finds Rick Moranis buying an unusual plant from a Chinese flower shop during a solar eclipse. It becomes apparent that this plant – Audrey II – is hungry for human blood and flesh, so Moranis initially obliges with his own blood, before offering up a dead Steve Martin. It's good fun. M. Night Shyamalan's *The Happening* is a little darker: here, humans and their polluting ways have become a threat to the planet, and plants start fighting back. They do this by releasing an airborne neurotoxin which gets into our brains and makes us want to kill ourselves. As a character in the film says, it's like an above-ground version of red tide syndrome – a real-life phenomenon that's been observed for the last few years in the Pacific Ocean, where harmful algal blooms have been producing toxins. If ingested in large quantities, these toxins have disturbing effects on human brain function, producing nausea, memory loss, seizures and even death. It's possible to imagine a scenario where plants might start producing new volatile compounds as a consequence of pollution. These new chemicals may then have an unexpected influence on humans… Fingers crossed that doesn't coincide with a blinding meteor shower.

Maybe the best evidence of all that we should fear the abilities of plants is that they have taken over the world – and are controlling us. Eighty-two per cent of the biomass on Earth is plant matter. It's their evolutionary triumph that is supporting animal life, not the other way around. We're sorry to tell you this, but they're not the parasites – we are.

Without plants, we would be absolutely screwed. Take the ascent of the mighty wheat plant, for example. If you believe that the best outcome for any living thing is world domination, then wheat is a real success story. Ten thousand years ago it was confined to the Middle East, jostling for position and resources among many other wild grasses. It was unremarkable, one of the pack. And yet it seduced us into inventing agriculture, and then spread itself across the globe.

Look at it this way: who's the big winner? The humans who are cultivating the wheat (and have since developed back problems and other ailments as a result) or the wheat itself? Before the agricultural revolution, humans were nomadic hunter-gatherers. Through a varied seasonal diet, their supplies were plentiful. But after they started farming, they became fixed in one place. They had to weed fields, plough the soil, sow seeds and carry water to seedlings. Basically, they had to carefully service every need of the wheat because they were utterly dependent on its crop. We became enslaved by our plant overlords. Know your place, feeble humans.

9

Hollywood Wants to Kill You... WITH OLD AGE!

'WHEN IT COMES TO THE END, YOU HAVE TO LET GO.'

— *The Curious Case of Benjamin Button* (2008)

David Fincher's *The Curious Case of Benjamin Button* is based on a short story by F. Scott Fitzgerald and follows the eponymous character, played by Brad Pitt, who ages in reverse. Though it sounds like it might be fun, it isn't: Benjamin's relationships are tricky and almost inevitably tragic. Nevertheless, humans have long been fascinated by slowing, stopping and ultimately turning back the biological clock, and, watching Benjamin's life unfold (refold?), it's hard not to feel a kind of envy. So, could we cheat time and reverse the ravages of ageing?

What Actually Is Ageing?

Benjamin Button was released on Christmas Day in 2008 and went straight to number two in the North American box office.

What beat it to the top spot?

Marley & Me, a romcom about a dog – starring Brad's ex, Jennifer Aniston.

Oh, that must have been a kick in the boys for Brad. Presumably *Button* was better received by the critics, though?

Yes, it got thirteen Oscar nominations and won three. That said, *Marley & Me* did get nominated for 'Best Liplock' at the Teen Choice Awards 2009.

Ah yes. The big one.

There's not much science in *The Curious Case of Benjamin Button*, we have to admit. Disappointingly, no one in the medical profession investigates why Benjamin's life runs backwards. The only attempt at an explanation comes from

Daisy, the love of his life, who believes the work of a blind French clockmaker called Monsieur Gateau has something to do with it. As a comment on the tragedy of the death of so many young men in the First World War, Mr Cake made a clock that runs backwards. It was installed at the New Orleans railway station just before Benjamin was born, and replaced just before Benjamin's death as a baby.

It's not much of an explanation, is it? But it does make us all think about the end. Even if we somehow manage to avoid premature death at the hands of killer robots, a viral pandemic, nuclear war, an asteroid, a plant – whatever, it doesn't really matter – there is one thing that is still guaranteed to get us. Old age – or, rather, the end of it. Even the term 'premature death' speaks to the crushing inevitability of it all. We all know death is coming eventually, and are just hoping to cling on for as long as possible.

The signs of our approaching demise are clear enough. We see them in others and then, gradually (and depressingly), we see them in ourselves. That's why everyone who saw Benjamin Button as a baby was so horrified: if you start life like that, what hope can there be? Well, knowing the answer to that question depends on what's really going on when we get old. And that's something we're still figuring out.

Aristotle, who bloody loved to think about stuff, reckoned that ageing was a gradual cooling of life's 'vital heat', until it was eventually extinguished. You can see why. It is a slow deterioration of function with time before the ultimate failure of function: death. But the funny thing about ageing – or to give it its fancy name, senescence – is that, at first glance at least, you'd have thought evolution would have got rid of it.

For a very long time the prime explanation for ageing and death was that it was making space. Death is something for the subsequent generations, ensuring there are enough resources for them to be reproductively successful, and thus benefiting the species as a whole. That doesn't quite work as an explanation though, for two related reasons. One is that evolution by natural selection only works on the level of the individual. It simply can't select for things that bring benefit to the species as a whole, so the idea of 'making room' for the next generation is something of a non-starter. The second problem is that, with all other things being equal, a long-living creature will have more offspring than a short-living one. That's essentially the ultimate goal of any biological creature, and the thing that evolution really does facilitate. A long-lived creature's increased reproductive success would mean its niche gets filled with organisms that are genetically predisposed to long lives. Death would recede over the horizon.

What compounds the problem is that 'natural' death is not a big part of the web of life anyway. In the natural world, most organisms don't die through ageing; it's extrinsic factors, like getting eaten by a predator, being out-competed for food,

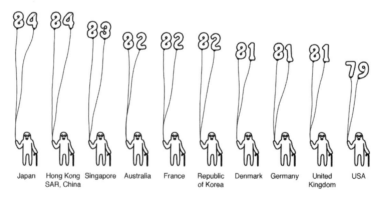

Japan | Hong Kong SAR, China | Singapore | Australia | France | Republic of Korea | Denmark | Germany | United Kingdom | USA

Human life expectancy has more than doubled since 1900 (source: World Bank)

having an accident, getting sick, dying during childbirth. All of these things mean that old age itself doesn't get to wield the reaper's scythe as often as you'd think. So most individuals will be dead long before they have to deal with the effects of ageing. Death-due-to-being-old just doesn't figure in evolution's shaping of species.

That becomes even more obvious when you realize that natural selection can't really act upon effects that emerge after reproduction has stopped – that is, in old age. No animal is rejecting a mate because it's seen what their potential mate's mother or father turned out like as they got older. This idea applies to both good and bad effects of ageing: the characteristics that result in a particular mate being selected might result in good or bad effects later on, but you can't allow for those effects at the time because you're blind to them. Taking the example of a genetic mutation that might result in an adverse effect in later life – the genetic contribution to Michael's receding hairline, say. It's likely that, by the time his long-suffering mate realizes that his healthy, lust-inspiring luscious locks are not going to last, this mutation will already have been passed on to the offspring. In cases like this, natural selection has no means of eliminating it from the population. It's also possible that these mutations would not become obvious because the organism doesn't reach old age. They would just silently lurk in the genome. If what gets passed to the next generation is something worse than receding hair – and there *are* worse things – the genetic line is going to be permanently compromised.

This idea forms the basis of the two main theories accounting for the evolution of ageing. They are actually very similar – in fact, they are likely to be operating in tandem. The first theory is called 'mutation accumulation'. As mentioned, a deleterious mutation that is only seen in later life would not be removed from the gene pool, and over time mutations like these would accumulate, producing what we describe as ageing effects.

The second theory is 'antagonistic pleiotropy'. Pleiotropic genes, or mutations, are ones which affect two or more traits or features. What this theory proposes is that you could have a mutation which has opposing effects in early life and later life. So it might be beneficial in early life (making you a great hunter, say) and increase reproductive success. Natural selection would favour this mutation and select for it. But then the same mutation has negative effects in later life (hair loss, say), when selection pressures are absent. So again, the unwanted, negative effects we associate with age will accumulate.

We'll look in more detail at the potential significance of senescent cells (these are cells which have stopped dividing) later on, but for now they provide an interesting example of natural selection's blindness to a late-showing negative effect. In early life, these cells can act as tumour suppressants and protect the body from cancer. This is a desirable effect, so evolution selects for it. But after a while these same cells can start to backfire – they become a cancer-causing agent, because they contribute to inflammation. To crudely paraphrase Obi-Wan Kenobi, they become the very thing they swore to destroy.

So, in summary, what actually is this thing we call ageing? It seems it is an accidental phenomenon where the body slowly loses the ability to repair itself. As with any machine that doesn't get regular maintenance, our bodies start to malfunction. Low-level inflammation spreads; our mitochondria – the little energy factories in our cells – work less well; some cells start multiplying uncontrollably (this is cancer); others just die and behave like zombies (these are the aforementioned senescent cells). Chromosomes get frayed and unravel. Our organs and tissues get clogged with organic rubbish. It's a total nightmare. But it's an accident, remember. As senescence researcher Tom Kirkwood once said, 'We know now that ageing is neither inevitable nor necessary.' We also know that, given sufficient care, accidents can be avoided. Can't they?

Is Ageing Inevitable?

> F. Scott Fitzgerald was a bit tame with the idea of a man that just ages backwards for no apparent reason.

> What do you mean?

> Well, there's a J. G. Ballard story called 'Mr F. is Mr F.' where a man reverts to infancy when his wife gets pregnant. But my absolute favourite is 'The Adventure of the Creeping Man' by Arthur Conan Doyle. An old fella wants to get his youthful libido back so injects himself with powdered monkey balls.

> And does it work?

> Yes and no. The libido's top-notch, but he turns into an ape.

> Isn't that the origin story for Harvey Weinstein?

> That is deeply offensive to our simian friends.

If we see ageing and death as accidents of biology that weren't engineered in by evolution, there is hope that we can undo the accident. If that sounds like a modern, crazy idea – you're right, it is. Because ageing is actually a modern problem.

For most of our history, we've been tackling the outside factors that kill us. We have implemented sanitation, vaccinations, medication, robust food supplies, surgery and so on. We've become so good at it that life spans in the developed world have more than doubled in the past 100 years. These days, we are living way beyond the ages we were reaching in our evolutionary past: old humans are a new thing!

So until now we simply haven't bothered tackling ageing itself – we have pretty much accepted it as inevitable. But that is starting to change. We can see the biological consequences of ageing as a problem to be solved, just as we solved the problems associated with the biological consequences of dirty drinking water.

Natural evolution certainly gives us hope. Take *Turritopsis dohrnii*, a species of hydrozoan (these are small marine creatures, the most famous example being the Portuguese man-of-war jellyfish). It has two distinct phases in its life cycle: its juvenile state as a polyp, and its adult state as a medusa, which looks a lot like a classic jellyfish. So far so normal. We see that kind of two-stage existence in lots of creatures, including butterflies and frogs. But this is where it gets freaky – physical damage, or environmental stress, cause the adult medusa to revert to its juvenile polyp. In due course it will return to being a medusa again. And this repeats, apparently indefinitely. There doesn't seem to be a limit to the number of resets it can do. In some senses, it is immortal. No wonder it's been dubbed the Benjamin Button Jellyfish. The mechanism for this is still being investigated but we know that as it rejuvenates, it is undergoing cellular transdifferentiation – one type of cells is being converted into another type of cells. How that might be harnessed in other creatures, no one knows. Yet.

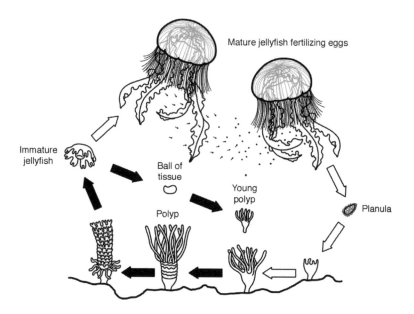

The immortal jellyfish can either reproduce normally or reverse its ageing and return to its immature state

The immortal jellyfish aren't the only death-defiers around. Planaria are a type of flatworm, and they are complex organisms – they have bilateral symmetry, a brain and other internal bodily structures. They are also the great regenerators of the animal kingdom. They can regrow their entire body from a single remaining piece, brain and all. This is mind-boggling on a lot of levels, not least because it appears that they can transfer some memories into their new brain after they are decapitated. But one consequence of special relevance here is that no one has ever seen an old planarian. They just continually repair and regrow their entire body throughout a seemingly endless lifespan.

Moving away from actual immortality, the lifespans of mice, worms and flies have been successfully and drastically extended using a variety of techniques including dietary (restricting calories) and genetic modifications (suppressing growth factor signalling genes). If it's not possible to do the same for us it would suggest that we were a strange outlier, separate from the rest of the natural world. That is surely unlikely.

But miracle life extension for humans won't happen without deliberate effort. Our average life expectancy has been steadily increasing for the last couple of centuries, but it does appear that the rate of increase is slowing, and will eventually come to a halt. It's believed that the oldest person to ever live reached 122. Not bad. France, Japan, the US and the UK have the largest number of 'supercentenarians' (a brilliant term meaning people who live to 110 or more). In those populations the maximum annual age of death (the age of the oldest person to have died in a given year) was increasing but since the 1990s has levelled out at around 115, even while average lifespan continued to increase. This suggests that, ignoring outliers who will always crop up, there is a 'natural limit' on human life at around 115. This ties in nicely with something called the Hayflick limit, which concludes that our maximum lifespan is about 120 years. Before Leonard Hayflick's work in the early 1960s, it had been assumed that normal human cells could keep on dividing forever. Hayflick demonstrated, by watching cells divide in petri dishes, that they could actually only undergo mitosis (cellular division and duplication) between forty and sixty times before some form of cellular death kicked in.

Ours is not a sudden death situation, of course. Unlike Hayflick's cells, we don't suddenly cease to function. What happens is that we spend somewhere around the last one-fifth of our lives fighting a rising tide of accumulating biochemical failures that create degenerative diseases. This state, known as 'late life morbidity', is bad news for everyone. The individual is dealing with more and more ageing-related afflictions, and society (not only in places where there is a welfare state) picks up the considerable bill. Eighty per cent of all healthcare costs in the USA are associated with chronic late-life diseases. If we don't come up with ways to slow, stop or reverse ageing, we might end up in a serious economic hole. Long-term care for the elderly and infirm is a challenge that isn't just going to go away. Between 2015 and 2030 it's estimated that the number of people on the planet aged sixty and over will jump from 900 million to one-and-a-half billion. By 2050 that number is projected to have topped two billion.

But many researchers feel we can counter this trend. There are two different, but linked, ambitions at play. The first is to just increase longevity; allow people to live longer. On its own, that's not so desirable – for the individual or society. The second is to increase 'healthspan': the proportion of life which is healthy and not plagued by the ill-effects of ageing. In recent years researchers have started to focus more on the latter. And you can see why: the thought of a disease- and pathology-free old age is very appealing. And potentially very lucrative indeed. So, given that there is no reason to doubt it could be possible, let's begin our run-down of all the avenues that are being explored.

How Can We Defeat Ageing?

> Benjamin's look as a child is based upon the latter stages of Hutchinson-Gilford progeria syndrome.

> Is that the awful disease where children look really old?

> Yeah. Brad Pitt had to spend five hours a day in the make-up chair.

> Welcome to my world.

B enjamin's adopted mother tells him that we're meant to lose the people we love. 'How else would we know how important they are to us?' Queenie asks. But it's a questionable perspective. We don't have to lose someone to know that they matter to us – and so we don't have to accept that senescence is just how things are meant to be.

As we saw earlier, as the clock ticks on, our bodies accumulate cells which have gone into senescence – they are worn out, have stopped dividing, cannot be repaired and just sit there. In earlier life they get cleared out, but not during old age. Worse, their presence is toxic: they destroy surrounding tissues and secrete proteins which contribute to low-level inflammation. They're bad news, in other words. It's been shown that introducing senescent cells from an old mouse into a young mouse will cause the younger mouse to age prematurely. And that's why we are developing 'senolytics', a type of drug that searches out and destroys these knackered old cells. So far, they seem promising. The first pilot trial in humans only occurred at the beginning of 2019, but the researchers described the results as 'preliminary but encouraging'.

Then there's fasting. This has long been used as an anti-ageing technique, and now it's being given a scientific makeover. Intermittent fasting and caloric restriction have extended lifespan and healthspan in test animals, probably because in tough times, when nutrient levels are low, cells are triggered to switch to a kind of energy conservation mode. This energy conservation means that minimal biochemical processing goes on – minimizing the processes that contribute to ageing. There is drug development in this area too: a group of drugs called rapalogs inhibit certain biological processes involved with metabolism – meaning it might be possible to trick the body into thinking it's fasting, with some knock-on anti-ageing benefits. One such compound – rapamycin – has been shown to lengthen the life of mice by 14 per cent, and there have been positive early trials with a similar drug in old people, which was shown to improve the function of their immune system.

Perhaps the creepiest, and certainly the most vampiric, of all the anti-ageing techniques being tested is the injection of young blood. Scientists were studying conjoined twins back in the 1970s and developed a particularly grim procedure called parabiosis, in which two animals (usually mice, of course) are stitched together so that they share a circulatory system and, therefore, blood. An unexpected result was that young mice joined to old ones aged prematurely, but crucially, the old mice were rejuvenated. There seemed to be a remarkable reversal of ageing in their lungs, bones, heart, brain and other organs.

The first human trials – admittedly on a very small group – have given reason for optimism. Patients with mild to moderate Alzheimer's were given weekly transfusions, for a month, of blood plasma – blood stripped of its red and white cells – from people aged eighteen to thirty. The control group were injected with a saline placebo. Although no significant effect on cognition was observed, there was noticeable improvement in 'daily living skills', and no serious adverse effects.

What makes these transfusions quite controversial is that currently it isn't clear how they are working – although several companies are looking to identify the 'active ingredients' within the plasma. One potential winner is the protein GDF11, the abundance of which declines with age. There are also blood proteins whose abundance increases with age, so other teams are looking at ways of blocking those. The likelihood is that the purported effects are being produced by a complex web of factors within the blood, so many experts are advising caution before proceeding further. Worryingly though, blood transfusions used for the treatment of dementia do not need FDA approval in the US, and some companies are jumping at the chance to turn young blood into money. At one symposium targeting rich old Floridian retirees, it's alleged that admission to a trial group would cost a cool $285,000. Another start-up in California is offering injections of youthful plasma for the bargain price of $8000.

If you're not a rich old Floridian, you could try working on your gut microbiome. It seems, from studies in both mice and humans, that the variety of bacteria in the gut diminishes with age. The mechanism for this is, again, a mystery. So what can we do with that information? How can we appropriately repopulate an old gut? Well, it's not for the squeamish.

Move aside blood transfusions and make way for a faecal transplant. Yes, you read that right. Researchers have done studies with turquoise killifish in which older fish have their natural gut flora cleared out by a course of antibiotics, and then swim around in water which has been contaminated with the faeces of younger fish. Naturally, the old fish ingest a bit of the young faeces, and the bacteria from that recolonize their gut.

Buyer beware

For all of the promise and encouraging results, most scientists are still very circumspect about when legitimate, proven anti-ageing therapies will be available. That's partly because the pharmaceutical industry has had its fingers burned before. In 2008, GlaxoSmithKline acquired a biotech company called Sirtris for $720 million – a chunk of change. They considered it to be worth it because the company had developed the first anti-ageing drug. Called resveratrol, and found in tiny quantities in red wine, it was widely regarded to be an absolute game-changer. The founder of Sirtris described the molecule as 'as close to miraculous' as you could get. But here's the kicker – in spite of its remarkable success in extending the lifespan of yeast (ha ha ha ha), it didn't work in humans. And in 2013 Glaxo wound the company up.

An interesting little coda to this cautionary tale is that resveratrol is now back in the running to be an anti-ageing hero. While senolytics destroy senescent cells, senomodifiers aim to nudge them out of their stupor and start dividing again. And, yes, some of the most promising senomodifiers are based on resveratrol…

So far, so gross. But here's where it gets really interesting. When the older fish were observed, they displayed activity levels more typical of a much younger fish. Not only that, their lifespans were increased by 37 per cent when compared to a control group that had their original old gut biome. So these fish were living longer and better. Before you get too excited and start pleading with spritely teenagers for a sample of their faecal waste, it should be strongly noted that these experiments have not been tried in any mammals, least of all humans.

You're no doubt waiting for us to mention stem cells. Right now you'd be hard-pushed to think of a medical condition that wasn't being treated with some form of stem cell therapy, and ageing is no different, it turns out. In some small trials of a procedure called mesenchymal stem cell (MSC) therapy, for example, frail elderly individuals were given just a single infusion of MSCs collected from the bone marrow of younger people. The researchers described the resulting physical improvements – in fitness and quality of life – as 'remarkable'.

Finally, we should mention epigenetic routes to rejuvenation. Epigenetic interventions can turn genes on or off, or make them more or less active. It's believed that the accumulation of epigenetic changes is a key factor in ageing, so researchers have done some genetic tweaking in – you guessed it – mice and were able to turn adult cells back to an embryonic-like state. They did this by activating four genes – so-called Yamanaka factors – for a brief period. A middle-aged mouse that underwent epigenetic tweaking saw damaged muscles and its pancreas rejuvenated.

This suggests something extraordinary. Not just the potential, through epigenetic tinkering, to slow down ageing, but the possibility of reversing it, Benjamin Button style. Imagine that: the ability to bring back youthful function. Your nana might just play football again. Well, maybe not your nana. Probably not even Michael. But, if the future of ageing research goes as planned, there's hope for Rick.

What Is The Future Of Ageing?

> Ageing isn't a fixed thing. I might be ten years older than you, but I'm ageing slower.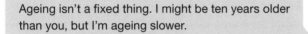

> Oh brilliant, you're going to talk about physics, aren't you?

> Yes. Because you're taller, your head is experiencing less of Earth's gravity than mine. Einstein's relativity says that makes its biological clocks tick ever so slightly faster.

> Well done Einstein.

> I'm not sure that works when you're talking about Einstein himself, an actual genius.

'I was thinking how nothing lasts, and what a shame that is,' Benjamin says to Daisy. It's no wonder he feels that way. He grew up (down?) in an old people's home that was, effectively, God's Waiting Room. There is an inevitability about death that makes us accept the notion that people at the end of long lives need care, rather than medicine. But should we accept that? One person who disagrees violently with that assertion is a man who does not accept that ageing is inescapable: Dr Aubrey de Grey.

De Grey believes there is someone alive today who will live to the ripe old age of 1000.* You could argue that he would say that: he runs a research facility in California called SENS. The acronym stands for Strategies for Engineered Negligible Senescence and has a rather pleasing tagline: 'Reimagine Ageing'. But for many decades he has been arguing that we have been making an entirely arbitrary, semantic distinction between the various elements of ageing. Some we label as diseases and are very keen to tackle. Others we label as, well, just ageing; these, for some reason, we choose not to address. De Grey aims to change that.

Of course, de Grey's assertion that someone alive now will live for a millennium is highly questionable. But he bases it on the idea that things like the Hayflick limit and the observed trends in human longevity do not take into account future developments in medicine. Yes, without further interference, there is almost certainly a limit to human lifespan. But you just know we *are* going to interfere, don't you?

As we have seen, in humans, we can divide the process of ageing into two components. The first is the creation of cellular damage, through our natural metabolic processes. The second is the accumulation of this damage in later life, which reaches a level that then causes problems, which we call pathology and age-related disease.

To tackle ageing, people have identified two general

---

* The birthday cake candle industry is, understandably, very excited about this.

strategies. First, we somehow break the link between metabolism and damage so that these processes no longer ultimately cause disease. Second, we make the body's cells more robust, so that they can handle more damage without descending into failure. Unfortunately both of these approaches are restrictively difficult. Our metabolic functions are extremely complex and we're only just beginning to understand them.

Luckily, de Grey is not bothered by these problems – because he is advocating a third path. Using the analogy of the way in which we keep man-made machines running for longer than they were originally expected to perform, he thinks we should be able to go in and periodically repair some of the cell damage, and thus prevent it from reaching a pathogenic level. This should be much simpler to achieve than trying to interfere with the causes (our metabolism) or the consequences (disease).

De Grey has identified seven different types of damage to be repaired, which can broadly be grouped into problems with the cells themselves, such as cancer, the overall loss of cells and senescent 'zombie' cells, and problems within the cells, such as the accumulation of junk biomaterials and malfunctioning mitochondria.

Such 'can-do' approaches to the fight against ageing go down well in Silicon Valley. That's why de Grey's SENS has had money from PayPal co-founder Peter Thiel (who once made the astonishingly banal observation that death is a 'terrible, terrible thing' that he prefers to fight). Other Silicon Valley firms on the same track include Calico, a company set up by Google and tasked with tackling ageing, and Unity Biotechnology, which has benefitted from the deep pockets in Amazon founder Jeff Bezos's finely tailored trousers. Meanwhile Mark Zuckerberg has been pumping billions into curing *all* disease, which is typically bold.

Do nothing, live longer

For those of us who would like to live a bit longer, in good health, but don't fancy going through the hassle of young blood injections, faecal transplants or starving ourselves, there may be some good news courtesy of a rodent. The Djungarian hamster – a popular pet – goes through a bizarre transformation during the winter months. It doesn't exactly hibernate, but it regularly goes into torpor – where its metabolic functions slow right down for several hours. During this period its grey fur turns white, it sheds some weight and its sex organs shrink. Nice.

When studied in the lab, hamsters in colder temperatures went into a deep torpor more frequently than those in warmer conditions. The really surprising thing is that during the hamsters' sleep, their telomeres grew longer.

Telomeres, which are caps of repetitive DNA at the end of our chromosomes, are meant to get progressively shorter with time. In fact, they shorten every time a cell divides. The common analogy is that they act like the ends of shoelaces, preventing the DNA from fraying, and there is apparently a correlation between length of telomeres and lifespan: animals, including humans, with short telomeres early in life, tend to have shorter lifespans and earlier onset of age-associated disease. But there is evidence that healthy lifestyle changes can regrow telomeres. Exercise in particular seems to protect them.

But the hamsters are rewriting this idea. The standard advice might have been to go for a run when you finish reading this chapter, but now we're not so sure. The colder the hamster's cage, the longer its telomeres grew during torpor. Great news for the integrity of the hamster DNA, and potentially their lifespan. So why not whack the air conditioning on full and get slumbering?

It's good that so many companies are trying to make anti-ageing drugs, because it increases the chances that one will be successful and develop a bona fide anti-ageing treatment that works and can be brought to market. Drug development is notoriously difficult. If the drugs don't fall at the mice-to-human hurdle (and around 90 per cent do, meaning that it's always worth scrutinizing bold headline claims in science journalism), then they're likely to fall at the actually-becoming-a-product hurdle. Very few drugs and treatments get anywhere near that far.

See also

Old people acting young plays well at the movies: who doesn't love *Cocoon*, where a group of seniors are helped out by friendly aliens with the power to rejuvenate their ailing bodies? Or there are the misbehaving residents of *The Best Exotic Marigold Hotel*, who discover life doesn't end with retirement. Those years are not always golden, though: *On Golden Pond* explores the destructive power of ageing and dementia, and earned Henry Fonda an Oscar. Similar themes won Julianne Moore an Oscar for her portrayal of dementia's cruel grip in *Still Alice*. Then there's *Nebraska*, which stars Bruce Dern as an ageing, confused, sweet but also bitter man fighting his family's attempts to put him in a retirement home. If you just want a bittersweet take on the agonies of ageing, Pixar's *Up* might be as good as it gets.

Nonetheless, we are finally at the stage of human history when fighting and maybe reversing ageing is a serious scientific goal, and that could be enough to save us. If you think that sounds ridiculous, consider this. When Aubrey de Grey talks about someone living to 1000, he isn't imagining them being given one treatment at sixty and – voila! – they live for another 940 years. He is, instead, confident of reaching a point he calls the 'longevity escape velocity'.

It's a fascinating idea. Imagine that in ten years' time, a sixty-year-old can be given a treatment which rejuvenates them by twenty years. This would mean that they weren't biologically sixty again until they were chronologically eighty. The problem of ageing would not have been completely solved at that stage, but it's entirely possible – probable, perhaps – that in the intervening twenty years more progress will have been made. That means the eighty-year-old, who is biologically sixty now, can opt for another, even better rejuvenation therapy. Maybe, given the progress that has happened, the same money buys them another thirty years. Now they are biologically fifty when their twenty-year maintenance cycle matures again on their 100th birthday. But again we have made progress (it's almost the twenty-second century, after all) and their biological clock now gets turned back forty years. They're effectively a teenager now. From here on in, they are only going to require occasional anti-ageing tweaks to escape the slippery descent into old age. Not quite a *Benjamin Button* scenario, but it's a very seductive theory nonetheless. And if anti-ageing researchers can deliver on its premise, it's a world-changer. Would you say no and go gently into that good night? No, neither would we.

10

Hollywood Wants to Kill You... WITH NUCLEAR ARMAGEDDON!

· ·

'THE DOOMSDAY MACHINE IS DESIGNED TO TRIGGER

ITSELF AUTOMATICALLY.'

— *Dr. Strangelove* (1964)

· ·

A whole raft of films look at the threat of nuclear war and its desolate aftermath, but surely the best example remains Stanley Kubrick's classic black comedy *Dr. Strangelove (Or: How I Learned to Stop Worrying and Love the Bomb).* Made over fifty years ago, during the Cold War, and set in 1964, it imagines a scenario in which a US general goes loopy and decides to launch an all-out nuclear attack on the 'Commies'. Why? Because (in his head) they are corrupting the 'precious bodily fluids' of Americans with fluoride. Towards the end, a character is seen riding an American H-bomb towards its Russian military target, wildly yee-hawing. Yes, it's a satire, but – shockingly – it turns out that this might be a rare implausible moment in the entire film.

What Is An Atomic Bomb?

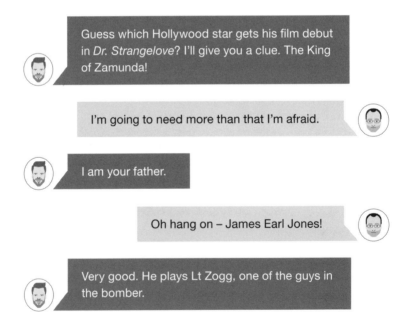

Guess which Hollywood star gets his film debut in *Dr. Strangelove*? I'll give you a clue. The King of Zamunda!

I'm going to need more than that I'm afraid.

I am your father.

Oh hang on – James Earl Jones!

Very good. He plays Lt Zogg, one of the guys in the bomber.

When nuclear bombs were first developed, some people weren't entirely sure that the technology was a total game-changer. They argued that the devastation of Hiroshima or Nagasaki was only equal to or less than the damage inflicted upon the German city of Dresden during the war. But Dresden was firebombed by hundreds of sorties over a period of time – the Japanese cities were each utterly destroyed by a single mission. As Albert Einstein put it, we were suddenly drifting 'towards unparalleled catastrophe'. A US military strategist commented in 1946 that the chief purpose of the military had been to win wars. 'From now on,' he said, 'its chief purpose must be to avoid them.' In many ways, *Dr. Strangelove* was Stanley Kubrick's contribution to that effort. Though devastatingly funny, the movie has serious roots: Kubrick read more than fifty books on nuclear weapons while preparing the script.

The first bit of business to address is the distinction between an A-bomb – the type of bomb that the US dropped on Japan in 1945 – and an H-bomb. The A-bomb, or atomic bomb, relies upon the release of energy produced by nuclear fission. This is the same principle on which nuclear power stations work. Heavy, radioactive elements like uranium and plutonium can be made to split into smaller atoms, and every split releases energy. The total mass of the resulting atoms is slightly less than the mass of the original atom, and the 'lost' mass is converted into energy – a lot of it. You'll probably remember Einstein coming up with what is now the world's most famous equation – $E=mc^2$ – which describes the equivalence of mass and energy.

Atomic bombs rely on pushing lots of these heavy atoms into one another, which causes them to split, releasing – among other things – high-energy neutrons that career into other atoms, causing those atoms to split. These then release more neutrons and cause more splitting: what we have here is a runaway chain reaction** that produces a huge blast of energy. The first and only A-bombs used in warfare, dropped on Hiroshima and Nagasaki, had yields equivalent to 14 and 18 kilotonnes of TNT respectively.

The other type – hydrogen bombs or thermonuclear bombs – use nuclear fusion and are far more powerful. Fusion is the same process that generates our sun's heat and light, so you could say we owe our very existence to it. But what fusion giveth, fusion may someday taketh away – unless we ensure the world's H-bombs remain unexploded.

Fusion involves the joining together of two or more smaller atoms, typically heavy isotopes of hydrogen like deuterium or tritium. In order to start a fusion reaction you have to input a lot of energy. So in fact H-bombs are two-bombs-in-one: a fission reaction in a primary component kicks things off, and there is a subsequent even larger fusion reaction in the secondary component. The fission reaction is the trigger, providing the energy required to get the fusion going. The mechanisms for this sort of energy transfer are strictly classified, for obvious reasons. In some bomb designs, rapidly moving neutrons, produced by the fusion, impact with the heavy atoms in the fission part and cause further splitting. And so the reactions fuel each other.

H-bombs were developed after the Second World War. The first one was tested by the US in 1952 and had a yield equivalent to 9000 kilotonnes of TNT. But it's believed – we don't really want to find out – that the explosions can be anything up to 1000 times as large as the biggest A-bombs. It's not just about the blast itself. The aftermath is, arguably, even more terrifying.

---

* Great film, hugely underrated. One for the next book? Pre-order now…

Size matters

During the Cold War the Russians, and the Americans, were desperate to assert their might by developing ever more monstrous thermonuclear weapons. The largest ever nuclear bomb was tested in 1961 by the Soviet Union. Nicknamed the Tsar's Bomb, it weighed in at 27 tonnes and was too big to fit inside the specially modified bomber that carried it, so the Soviets strapped it to the underside of the fuselage. It was dropped, on a massive parachute, over an archipelago in the Barents Sea, in the far north of the USSR. Upon detonation it released the energy of around 52 million tonnes of TNT. That's nearly 4000 times more powerful than the A-bomb that devastated Hiroshima. A village on the archipelago 34 miles from ground zero – the point on the Earth's surface closest to the detonation of the weapon – was flattened.

What's even more extraordinary about this bomb is that it was supposed to be bigger. One of the Russian scientists tasked to build it was Andrei Sakharov. He came up with a layered weapon he called the *sloika* – a layered cake. Each layer was separated by uranium, which would also undergo fission upon detonation. The estimated power of it was 91 million tonnes of TNT. Sakharov was worried that testing this device would result in catastrophic radioactive fallout across the USSR so he modified the design, replacing the uranium layers with lead to reduce the intensity of the nuclear reactions. Many people believe that the Tsar's Bomb was one of the reasons that two years later, in 1963, the Partial Test Ban Treaty was signed, thus ending the period of atmospheric testing. To this day, no weapon has ever been created with comparable power, and nuclear testing is only done underground.

When we detonate a 14-kilotonne A-bomb over a city, the temperatures at ground zero will reach tens of millions of degrees. The energy is not just given out in the form of heat: there is also a blast wave, which causes a ripple of immense air pressure and high-speed winds. Then there's the radiation. Within a radius of several hundred metres everything will be vaporized. A fireball forms and rises, cooling as it does so, and expands to form the familiar mushroom cloud. Contaminated debris falls from the cloud over a vast area around the blast centre, creating the deadly radioactive fallout. The immediate, local effects are severe. Depending on the population density, tens, maybe hundreds, of thousands of people die. But the longer-term effects end up killing far more people.

In the 1980s, scientists including Carl Sagan first started to look at the possibility of nuclear war plunging the planet into a 'nuclear winter'. They realized that there must be similarities between the impact of a large meteor – such as the one that hit Mexico and wiped out the non-avian dinosaurs (see Chapter 2) – and even a 'small-scale' nuclear war. Such a war might involve, say, a tit-for-tat exchange of 100 explosions in cities, each of 14 kilotonnes.

NASA scientists have used sophisticated climate models to examine the effect of an exchange like this. Around 5 megatonnes of soot – black carbon particles – would be injected into the upper atmosphere by the resulting urban firestorms. Once there, they would block out the sun's rays and continue to influence atmospheric temperature and surface temperature for up to a decade. Global temperatures would drop to such an extent that it would constitute a mini ice age. Not only that, but precipitation rates (rainfall, basically) would drop and the protective ozone layer would be depleted, allowing more of the dangerous UV light from the sun to reach the planet's surface.

These after-effects are truly global: when it comes to nuclear war, there's really no such thing as 'keeping out of it'. A regional nuclear conflict still has the potential to create global environmental effects that cause crops to fail and millions of people to starve – and, potentially, develop cancer, fertility problems and other sicknesses thanks to the long-term increase in irradiation. It really is to be avoided…

How Have We Avoided Nuclear Armageddon So Far?

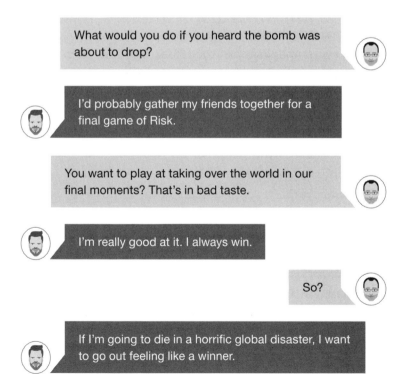

In the film, Dr Strangelove is baffled to find out about the existence of the secret Russian Doomsday Machine. As he says, 'The whole point... is lost if you keep it a secret!' What point? He's talking about game theory.

After the 1968 Non-Proliferation Treaty, only five nations had nuclear weapons – the US, the USSR, France, the UK and China. In the last couple of decades that has expanded to include India, Pakistan, North Korea and, unofficially, Israel. Even though the numbers have fallen since the 1980s, there are still tens of thousands of warheads spread across the world. So how have we managed to avoid nuclear war for so long?

There have certainly been some close shaves, but it all ultimately comes down to deterrence and the cheery idea of MAD – mutually assured destruction.

MAD was first posited in the 1950s, at a time when people hadn't yet considered the deadly aftereffects of the smoke and consequent climate effects. Nevertheless, they realized that if two or more nuclear powers go at each other, retaliating with full force, it doesn't matter whether you get the first strike in. Such is the power of the weapons that everyone will be utterly destroyed. As Dr Strangelove himself puts it, 'Deterrence is the art of producing in the mind of the enemy the fear to attack.'

It all feels a bit like a very risky game, doesn't it? And that's how researchers have modelled it, using a branch of mathematics known as game theory. This allows us to look at cooperation and conflict between rational decision makers (there are, of course, question marks over how many of the decision makers with fingers hovering over metaphorical red buttons are rational). Game theory started out as a way of examining the outcomes of games of chance and skill like poker, but since the 1940s it has been applied to warfare, and potential warfare. It allows analysis in situations where your best decision depends on what the other player does, and vice versa. You set out who the protagonists are, what they each know, what they want, what they are able to do and what the possible outcomes are. This results in a stripped back, logical outline of the situation. What it doesn't always do is provide a path to the endgame, or the desired outcomes.

There's a simple example of this which is known as the prisoner's dilemma. Here, two criminals have been arrested (let's call them Rick and Michael). If they both stay silent under questioning in their separate cells, they will be released. But can they trust each other to do that? If Rick confesses and Michael doesn't, Rick will get a short sentence while Michael gets a longer one. So Rick is tempted to confess, just in case Michael confesses first. The same is true the other way around: Michael might benefit from confessing, in case Rick breaks under pressure. The big dilemma is that if they both implicate the other, they'll both get a heavy sentence.

The best outcome is for neither of them to talk. But that involves trust that just isn't there. There is no easy answer. The options in a nuclear war (and indeed, any war) are – attack or not attack. If this was a one-time deal, game theory will tell you that the most reliable, rational strategy is to attack – or in the prisoner's dilemma, confess and betray your mate. But this is not a one-off unless you can neutralize the enemy's threat with your first attack (we'll get to that). This is a longer-term interaction. There will be retaliation.

In the prisoner's dilemma, that's equivalent to there being not just one round of questioning, but many, with the stakes changing depending on how the previous round has gone – Rick has the potential to retaliate if Michael betrays him. With the possibility of retaliation hanging over you, you can't just play in your short-term interest: you have to make decisions that make sense in the long term. So the strategy should shift to cooperation. That's also the optimal nuclear strategy.

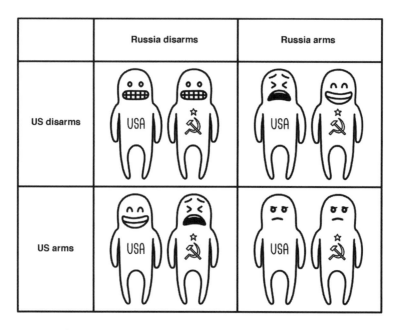

Game theory says that neither side will be particularly happy if both are arming or disarming. But an imbalance is even worse

Keeping the threat of retaliation credible is part of the reason given to justify the unchecked stockpiling of nuclear weapons during the 1970s and 1980s by Russia and the US. Game theory also predicts this – given both sides have the choice between arming and disarming, even though both disarming would really be the best outcome (no chance of nuclear war; massive expenditure avoided), they won't risk ending up disarming while the opponent arms, and therefore being vulnerable to annihilation. So both will continue with their armaments…

There is one assumption in all of this: you have to believe your opponent will retaliate. And that's why Strangelove has such a problem with the Russian Doomsday Machine being a secret. It was an automated retaliatory system: if a strike was launched against Russia, it would be detected and immediately trigger a devastating counter-attack, destroying the entire world without any human decision-making. It's a horrendous prospect, enough to make you stop and think before pressing the button that launches an attack on Russia. But it can only deter you if you know about it.

In an incredible stranger-than-fiction development, Russia started working on a set-up almost exactly like this in the 1970s. It was called the Dead Hand system and would allow the firing of retaliatory nukes if no high-up Russian officials could be consulted quickly enough.* And they kept it secret for years – meaning that it didn't count as a deterrent. Not everyone understands the rules, it seems.

But here's where you can actually unbalance this whole dangerous game. You might know about the deterrent, but have a plan to neutralize it. If you can launch what's known as a counterforce strike – an attack that knocks out the opponent's nuclear capabilities – then there is no deterrent, and you can strike with impunity.

To avoid this scenario, Russia and the US have spread their nuclear weapons around, ensuring they are ready to go

---

* Although it had the requisite sensors, it's believed that this system was never completely automatic.

from land, air and sea. Submarines with nuclear weapons are quietly gliding around the oceans, for example. These are hard to track, and therefore not easy to knock out. Not that people aren't trying: there are rumours that various nations are developing ways of spotting and tracking a submarine's turbulent wake. Still, the idea remains solid: if your enemy hits your land-based nukes, you can always call upon your subs or your planes to punch back.

The big problem with all of this is that it encourages an arms race in measures and countermeasures. Your enemy is always working on a way to destroy or disable your deterrent, and so you have to do the same. After all, if one side were to arrive at a stage where technology allows reliable detection and elimination of the other side's weapons, a first strike becomes a viable and winnable course to take. As a result, the main winners so far are the companies that research, develop, build and sell the offensive and defensive technologies. It's far from ideal, but – on the plus side – at least we're all still here. So far, so good. Or is it?

How Safe Are We Now?

A guy called Thomas Schelling literally wrote the book on game theory as applied to nuclear war – called *The Strategy of Conflict*.

Yes, and he was a consultant on *Dr. Strangelove*.

Not only that, he won a Nobel Prize.

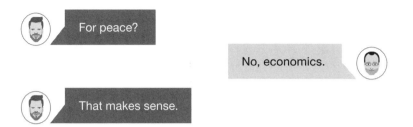

E ver heard of the Doomsday Clock? It's the depressingly named creation of a group called the Bulletin of the Atomic Scientists, who set it up to show how close we are to annihilation. The idea is that the closer the Doomsday Clock's hand is to midnight, the more imminent is the threat of global disaster.

It started at seven minutes to midnight in 1947. In 1953 it got the closest it's ever been, two minutes to midnight, when the Soviets tested a thermonuclear device just a year after the US had tested the first. At a time of relative peace, the end of the Cold War and dissolution of the Soviet Union in 1991, it moved out to seventeen minutes. But, just recently, it's moved much closer again. North Korea's transition to a nuclear state saw the hand tick forward in January 2018 from two-and-a-half to two minutes to midnight, where it remains today – we've equalled the record! It's stayed at this precarious position for the last two years.

Exactly how these movements are decided upon is a little vague, but we know that the board take into account a whole range of factors, of which the threat of nuclear war is just one. The potential of catastrophic climate change is another. They believe that the global nuclear order 'has been deteriorating for many years', and 2018 was particularly bad, for reasons we'll come to later.

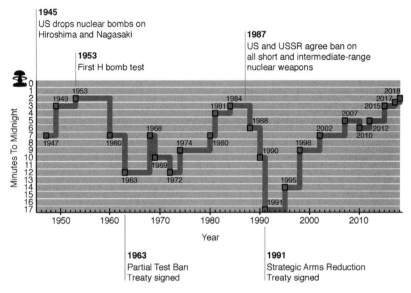

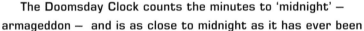

The Doomsday Clock counts the minutes to 'midnight' — armageddon — and is as close to midnight as it has ever been

There has always been a tension with the US nuclear command and control, and it's described as always/never. On the one hand, it is essential that you *always* have the capability to use your weapons immediately in wartime, in order for them to work as a deterrent. On the other hand, you *never* want them to be accidentally or involuntarily fired in peacetime. These are clearly competing and contradictory aims. Many of the administrative and technical measures you can think of to make the first requirement hold, turn out to make the second requirement harder to achieve – and vice versa.

There are two distinctly different situations in which someone decides to launch a nuclear strike. The first is where, having been monitoring the activities of their enemies, the military decide that there is an urgent threat. Maybe they suspect an enemy is about to launch a nuclear strike of their own – or just has. In this case they involve the President, who decides whether to go along with what he is being advised. If he does, the nuclear strike will proceed.

Ideally the President would consult with his National Security Advisors before making the call, but that is not actually necessary. This is a very streamlined process, designed in the days of the Cold War to ensure launch orders could be transmitted extremely quickly. There's no time for dilly-dallying if a nuke-laden intercontinental ballistic missile is winging its way over to you from Siberia.

The second full escalation scenario is altogether more alarming. In this one, the President decides on his own that it is time to unleash nuclear 'fire and fury like the world has never seen'. He puts a call into the military and tells them that. The fortunate thing here is that the military are well-drilled in rejecting illegal orders. If the President were to attempt something like this without prior consultation with his senior advisors, alarm bells would be ringing (both figuratively and literally). The national security team would be alerted and the President would need to convince them to take this course of action. This would, at the very least, take a bit of time.

But it's not only poor decision-making we should fear. These days there is a new worry: it is now possible that an enemy could hack into a command and control system and disrupt it from within. That's true even if it's not connected to the Internet.

The first, and probably most famous, example of such a hack was the digital weapon Stuxnet – a virus that broke new ground by doing real-world, physical damage. It caused the failure of many of Iran's uranium-enrichment centrifuges, a vital component of their nuclear programme.* To prevent such interference, all of the equipment was 'air-gapped' – separated from the Internet, exactly as nuclear command and control systems are. But the attackers (most likely to be an off-book collaboration between the US and Israel, although that's never been confirmed) knew that they could get around this if they were able to put the virus on to a USB stick which was then plugged into the centrifuge control equipment. So they set about infecting the computers of five different contractors who they knew would be working at this Iranian nuclear facility. The virus sat dormant in these computers, waiting for a USB stick to appear. It jumped on, but only became active when that USB stick was introduced to the target equipment. Job done. It took a very long time for the Iranians to figure out what had happened.

We also think there was some more cyber-meddling in 2016, when a UK Trident missile test went wrong. Somewhat terrifyingly, it started mistakenly heading towards the US, but quickly self-destructed when it recognized the error. No official government line has been given on what caused the problem, but it does look consistent with some form of software attack. Trident systems are, again, entirely separate from the Internet. However, the submarine that launched the missile had just had a refit during which it had been worked on by multiple subcontractors. That seems like the perfect opportunity for a Stuxnet-like piece of interference.

This kind of thing isn't going away any time soon, by the way. Much of the US command and control system is antiquated – bits of it still have floppy discs – but it's all being upgraded. Some people fear that the complexity of the

---

* Of course, they're not meant to actually have one, the rascals!

replacements may actually just provide a clutch of unanticipated back doors for hackers. They are a resourceful bunch, after all.*

Did Trump Make Things Better Or Worse?

> Mutually assured destruction inspired my first ever career choice.

> You wanted to study the maths of game theory?

> No, I wanted to be a fighter pilot, but without the risk of dying in combat. I figured that MAD meant no more wars.

> That prediction didn't work out, did it? Well, at least I got to work in game theory.

> What do you mean? You're a game show host.

> Exactly. I have to explain the theory behind the game to all the contestants.

The opening slate of *Dr. Strangelove* shows a disclaimer: 'It is the stated position of the US Air Force that their

---

* As you'll know if you've seen *Hackers*.

safeguards would prevent the occurrence of such events.' This may not be true.

A former military analyst called Daniel Ellsberg – most well-known for leaking the Pentagon Papers, as depicted in the Steven Spielberg film *The Post* – has spoken extensively about the ability of a lone general to launch a nuclear strike. The nuclear command and control set-up in the US was not, as many believed, solely in the hands of the President. Far from it, in fact: in the 1960s, the US Air Force's chief of staff General LeMay, who was in charge of Strategic Air Command (and said of *Dr. Strangelove* 'Nothing like that could ever happen'), had ultimate control over the deployment of the air force's nukes. There were also plans in place to wipe out Russia (and China, on the basis that they might as well get shot of as many communists as possible in one go). This would have seen nuclear launches against every Russian city with a population of 25,000 or more. In other words, total annihilation.

Now there's another lone man to fear. A significant reason the Doomsday Clock is so close to midnight at the time of writing is because of the Orange One. Well-qualified people have expressed significant concerns about President Donald Trump's suitability and fitness to be the man with his finger on the nuclear button. Harvard University professor of public health Frederick Burkle, for example, has suggested that Trump (and Kim Jong-un and Vladimir Putin) have shown signs of antisocial personality disorder. That would mean they would have little interest in peace and plenty of interest in continuing conflict. Some experts certainly feel that Trump could, acting entirely on his own, impulsively initiate a nuclear war. Let's examine just how valid those fears are.

Madness is a big feature in *Dr. Strangelove*. But in the real world, it may not always be a bad thing. In fact, in the MAD scenario we have to deal with where nuclear arsenals are concerned, it can have an extremely positive effect. Yes, Trump's seemingly unhinged, unpredictable dealings with North Korea in 2017 may have terrified us all. But some behavioural theorists reckon this approach is, counter-intuitively, a very sensible way of dealing with the situation.

Your cut-out-and-keep guide to nuclear survival

1 Move to the Marshall Islands in the North Pacific.

2 OK, that doesn't seem practical. Go and stay with friends in Switzerland – by law, every home has to either have a nuclear bunker or access to one.

3 If you're anywhere near ground zero – which you shouldn't be, you should be on a remote island or in a Swiss bunker – tempting as it may be to gawp, do not look directly at the blast. It'll blind you.

4 Find shelter as soon as possible, and stay there. Being in the middle of a building is much better than being outside.

5 Take all of your clothes off and throw them away – they'll be harbouring radioactive material.

6 Have a nice long shower, if available. Don't rub too hard, you don't want to break the skin.

7 For God's sake, just move to the Marshall Islands.

It's actually called the 'madman strategy' – and the US has used it before. Richard Nixon pulled it on the Russians in the late 1960s: the Americans were deliberately leaking information to their Russian counterparts, pretty much saying that they couldn't control the President, and that he was irrational and impulsive. Why would this be a good technique? Well, game theory says that you have to look at the possible outcomes. Really, there are only two – conflict or some sort of bargained compromise.

In the present day, the best result for the US is the bargained compromise: North Korea agrees to scale back its nuclear programme, or even shelve it. But to drive this bargain, the US needs their threats – to make a first nuclear strike against North Korea – to seem credible. After all, a pre-emptive first strike for the US would clearly not be in America's national interest: it has the potential to escalate into a full-scale nuclear war and result in thousands, if not millions, of casualties – including the US's allies in South Korea, who would be sitting ducks. Rationally, it's clear this decision would never be taken, which means that giving the appearance of irrationality is the only way of making the threat seem real.

Interestingly, North Korea appears to be using a similar strategy, because the same argument can be applied to its position. Even more so, in fact, because it doesn't even have the nuclear arsenal to back up its threats: it would be so insanely outgunned that its threats seem doubly reckless.

Whatever the truth behind these strategic positions, there's a sweet little spin-off benefit for both leaders. Trump's aggressive posturing seems to go down well with his Republican voter base, and he can always explain the real-world lack of action as being down to his hands being tied by the annoying checks and balances of Congress and so on. For Kim Jong-un, he can point to the absence of US military action as a great victory – he's played chicken with a world superpower, and it has backed off.

The situation between the US and North Korea is volatile: at the time of writing, it appears to have settled down and Trump and Kim Jong-un seem to be on relatively friendly terms. However, that could change in an instant.* After all, North Korea continues to develop its weapons capabilities, and numerous other developments warrant concern.

Firstly, in 2018, the US pulled out of the Joint Comprehensive Plan of Action, which has maintained serious constraints on Iran's nuclear programme and been a major success in terms of non-proliferation. By February 2019, the US was reportedly planning to withdraw from a treaty which bans 'intermediate range' missiles. This implies that weapons that have been banned for a long time might come back into play. Thirdly, the various nuclear powers are all engaged in modernization programmes that look to sensible observers like a return to a global nuclear arms race. The previous ambitions to reduce or constrain nuclear forces appear to have evaporated. Lastly, looking at the military doctrines and approaches of the US and Russia, it seems that where there was previously an effort to minimize the role of nukes in defence planning, there is now an increasing focus on actually deploying them.

On top of all this, we are entering an era of dogged innovation in nuclear weapons themselves. President Obama's aim to set an example to the world by reducing the US number of warheads didn't exactly go to plan. The Russians and Chinese modernized their weaponry in response.

---

* Just to make our lives difficult it seems; at the time this is going to print, the relationship is deteriorating again. How is it now, as you're reading this?

See also

Almost every angle of the nuclear threat has been covered by Hollywood. There's John Woo's *Broken Arrow*, which gets its title from a bit of US military terminology used when a nuclear weapon goes missing or is accidentally detonated. For some reason Woo decided against 'Empty Quiver', which is another genuine, and suitable, piece of US jargon, and an undeniably great name for a film. *The China Syndrome* is most notable for its sinister foreshadowing: it's about a cover-up of an incident at a nuclear power plant, and was released in cinemas, in 1979, just twelve days before a real-life disaster – the Three Mile Island accident in Pennsylvania, where a reactor suffered a partial meltdown. *The Hunt for Red October*, based on the Tom Clancy novel, follows the defection of a Soviet nuclear submarine with a 'caterpillar drive' that renders it undetectable by US sonar. It also features a Russian accent from Sean Connery that lives long in the memory, and stars James Earl Jones, who evidently loves a nuclear theme. And then there's the 1983 classic *WarGames*, which sees Matthew Broderick's young hacker get into a US supercomputer and run a simulation of a nuclear war – which turns out not to be a simulation. There is a long-standing rumour that then-President Reagan was inspired by the film to create the first Presidential directive on computer security.

It's no longer a numbers game. This arms race is about novelty, and tactical and technical innovations. The Russians have been developing an underwater drone which could enter an enemy harbour and detonate a 'dirty bomb', contaminating a city with sickness-inducing levels of radiation. As already mentioned, if you have these capabilities, you want people to know about it – it's believed that the Russians deliberately leaked these plans. By demonstrating another possible form of retaliation to a first strike by the US, they keep the deterrence alive and well.

Meanwhile, the North Koreans are close to having an intercontinental ballistic missile (ICBM) capable of hitting the US mainland. So, following the classic trajectory of these things, Trump and his military advisors are investing heavily in their weapons, anxious to ensure that they retain a credible threat in the face of their potential adversaries' improved arsenal. In Trump's words, they're after a nuclear proposition 'so strong and powerful that it will deter any acts of aggression'.

One particularly spicy development is a change in US policy regarding when a nuclear strike might be authorized. For decades the trigger has always been a perceived imminent or actual nuclear attack from an enemy. Now, however, cyber-attacks are mentioned. The US has said that it might respond to a serious attack on critical infrastructure (mobile phone networks or the power grid, for example) with the nuclear option. Opponents think this is entirely disproportionate. It does sound a bit excessive. But would you want to find out if they're bluffing?

As a result of all this, the Bulletin of the Atomic Scientists believes that the world is once again headed towards a global unregulated nuclear environment the likes of which hasn't been seen for decades. It's calling this the 'new abnormal': a 'pernicious and dangerous departure from the time when the United States sought a leadership role in designing and supporting global agreements that advanced a safer and

11

Hollywood Wants to Kill You.... WITH DEATH!

'PHILOSOPHY FAILED. RELIGION FAILED. NOW IT'S

UP TO MEDICAL SCIENCE.'

— *Flatliners* (1990)

As we've seen, plenty of movies look into causes of death – but what about the movies that deal with death itself? There's no shortage of them: our fascination with death – and what comes after it – means that stories exploring the process and aftermath of a demise are a guaranteed win for movie producers. Look at *Ghost*, for example. On second thoughts, don't: look at Joel Schumacher's 1990 classic *Flatliners*. It features Kiefer Sutherland, Julia Roberts, Kevin Bacon, Billy Baldwin and Oliver Platt as a group of medical students deliberately walking the line between life and death – just to see what lies beyond this mortal experience. They take it in turns to have their hearts stopped for minutes at a time before being resuscitated (hopefully) so they can report back. *Flatliners* takes us into the fascinating science of near-death experiences, the ethics of resuscitation and the definition of death itself. What a way to end it all...

How Do We Define 'Dead'?

> At the risk of sounding like I have an obsession with film characters' coats, I'm a big fan of Kiefer Sutherland's trench.

> Of course you are: trench coats are Hollywood's shorthand for characters who are in control.

> Yes. Keanu Reeves in *The Matrix*. Humphrey Bogart in *Casablanca*.

> Exactly. Ever rocked one?

> Of course. You?

I bought one once, but it didn't really work.

 O I imagine it was more Columbo than Neo, wasn't it?

Death is not something we are generally comfortable with. Bring it up in conversation and you'll find it puts people on edge, or makes them change the subject with telling speed. That's what makes Kiefer Sutherland's Nelson such an interesting character. He is, unlike most of us, willing to stare it full in the face. 'I don't want to die,' he tells his classmates. 'I want to come back with answers.' And so they kill him.

Or do they? Does he actually die? 'Are we in the room with a dead man?' asks Billy Baldwin's character. It's an interesting question.

Occasionally, you might come across a thing that was alive but is now definitely dead – some roadkill, perhaps, or the mosquito you just pummelled into your thigh. Doctors, on the other hand, often have to make a judgement call. Sometimes, they have to make an arbitrary decision about whether a patient is alive or dead, and whether it is OK to stop trying to restore them to health. We know it's an arbitrary decision because we keep changing our minds about where that line is.

Perhaps aware of this, and wanting to avoid burying or burning someone alive, the Greeks and Romans used to err on the side of caution. They would wait three days for putrefaction to start; only once there was a bit of rotting going on would they start the funeral procedures. The Romans put in an extra safeguard, cutting a finger off the corpse to see if there was any blood flow, then calling out the deceased's name three times. If there was no response (and it's hard to believe there ever was at this point in the proceedings), they would go ahead and light the funeral pyre.

Eventually, people got bored of waiting for a good funeral. By medieval times, people were a bit more savvy about biological realities. They would check for a heartbeat, for instance, and hold a mirror up to the person's mouth. If the mirror clouded, there was breath, not death. If there was a heartbeat, or a pulse, you could not in all good conscience say they were a goner. Otherwise, they were fair game for the funeral guy.

Not that people were entirely comfortable even with this – especially when there were epidemics or battles that meant burials might be rushed. Maybe that's why George Washington asked for Greek-style patience before his funeral. On his deathbed he said, 'Have me decently buried, but do not let my body be put into a vault in less than two days after I am dead.' By the nineteenth century people had started to request 'safety coffins' that contained a string you could pull if you suddenly woke up 6 feet under. The string would ring a bell on the surface. It's hard to know how you'd feel about hearing it if you were visiting the grave at the time, but no doubt the London Association for the Prevention of Premature Burial would thank you for adding another example to justify its existence.

New safety coffin designs were being registered right up to the 1950s. The demand for them started to drop away at that time perhaps because doctors, rather than declaring you dead when you weren't, were more likely declaring that you were alive when you – maybe – weren't. By the 1960s, life-support technologies were making declarations of death ever more difficult.

And here you can start to see the problem we have created for ourselves. Nowadays, hospitals are crammed with people who stop breathing without anyone declaring them dead. That's because in many cases we can do the work of breathing for them. It's a similar story with the heart. Yes, it can stop and – if left alone – the owner will die (though the heart will sometimes spontaneously restart). But we have developed techniques for pumping the chest to keep blood flowing around the body, or actually restarting the heart with a jolt of electricity, as happens so many times in *Flatliners*. In other words, a flatline on the electrocardiogram doesn't mean you're dead.

The development of medical technologies that could alter the 'vital signs' created huge dilemmas for doctors in the 1960s. Take the artificial respirator, for instance. Suddenly, someone who had stopped breathing for themselves could now have their blood artificially oxygenated. What was previously a fast track to lethal brain damage was no longer a problem; if their heart was still beating, all their organs would continue to function with this oxygenated blood. But is someone who can't live independently of a machine definitely alive? People with amyotrophic lateral sclerosis (ALS), spinal cord injuries and other conditions that make life-support technologies vital would argue if you said no.

As far as the heart is concerned, defibrillation is a huge success story in restarting the heart's muscle contractions. But how long should you persevere if it doesn't seem to be working? In 1997, a US Institutes of Health report said that death became official five minutes after the heart stopped beating. But in 2013, an American Heart Association report suggested doctors should continue cardiopulmonary resuscitation for thirty-eight minutes after the heart stops, then declare the patient properly dead.

Given the conflicts, it's no surprise that we have shifted our focus away from the heart and lungs, and on to the brain. If there's no brain activity, that must be death, surely? It seems obvious, but even here there is plenty of controversy. How do you define brain activity?

In April 2019, a team of researchers at Yale University supplied oxygen and nutrients to the brain of a pig that had been dead for four hours. Astonishingly, this provoked some brain cells into functioning again: for the next thirty-six hours, these cells metabolized sugars and made proteins. No one knows whether such a process could restore consciousness – the team deliberately prevented consciousness from arising using a chemical that blocked the neurons from firing. But when the researchers removed bits of the brain tissue and jolted them with electricity, neurons did fire. Perhaps even more weirdly, we've seen brain cells grown in a dish produce human-like brainwaves. They were similar in form to those produced by a premature baby. Signals of brain activity are not everything.

Nonetheless, these days we define death by the signals emanating from the brain, using the 'irreversible cessation of functioning of the entire brain, including the brainstem' as the point of no return. In this state, there is no prospect of the patient ever breathing without mechanical assistance. But this 'whole-brain' death doesn't give the whole story.

For starters, you can damage small parts of the brain in a way that means the unfortunate owner will never recover consciousness. And advances in technology mean you can now find life-confirming brain activity in people who, a few decades ago, would have been declared dead. What's more, we have seen that even fully functioning parts of the brain can sometimes show no electrical activity. In the 1970s, a study showed that you can get EEG signals out of a lump of gelatin if you're not careful about how you define a 'signal'. Add that to the fact that the bodies of whole-brain-dead patients can be maintained in a way that means all their other organs are healthy and viable, and you can start to see that defining 'dead' is not as easy as it once might have been.

The case of Jahi McMath provides a perfect example: in 2013, she was admitted to a hospital in Oakland, California, for an operation to improve her breathing while asleep. A while after surgery, the thirteen-year-old suffered massive blood loss and cardiac arrest. The hospital's doctors declared her brain dead and started proceedings to take her off life support. Things might have been different in other states, where religious beliefs often influence legislation, but the state of California issued a death certificate. However, the family's lawyers asked for the certificate to be revoked and for life support to continue. Jahi's family flew her body to New Jersey, where state legislature means that families can reject a declaration of brain death if it conflicts with their religious beliefs. They treated Jahi as if she were alive, even singing to her on her birthdays, until she began to suffer liver and kidney failure in 2018 – while still on life support. The family believe she only died on 22 June 2018. The California hospital sets the date of death in 2013.

That's why some medical ethicists are suggesting that we each create our own definition. They reckon that, at the point where medical professionals no longer agree, you could decide if your life should be considered as over and done with. Then you write those criteria down and make sure they're part of your medical records so that everyone can respect your decision. Are you dead? You tell us.

Life after death

There's a thorny problem with our increasing ability to keep people alive: it has become ever harder to find viable organ donors. Fewer than 1 per cent of human deaths now happen in a way that provides transplantable organs.

One of the solutions is to shift the emphasis on the definition of death. That's because the outcome of transplants after circulatory death are much better than those that take place after brain death. This has led to a situation where, in some cases, we are harvesting organs from people who might still be described as technically alive.

It's called 'donation after circulatory death', and the idea is that people's hearts have stopped beating and won't start again. They are no longer breathing, either, so there is no chance that they will spontaneously spring back to life. And then, after a certain length of waiting time – five minutes in the UK, two minutes in the US, twenty minutes in Italy, for example – they are connected to a machine that keeps the blood oxygenated and circulating, so that their organs remain fresh and viable.

There is often still some brain activity while all this is going on, and surgeons might choose to insert a barrier that prevents oxygenated blood from reaching the brain. A lot of people find this pretty tricky ethical ground: it sounds like the doctors are doing their utmost to ensure the patient can't recover, while making them a perfect donor for someone else's new organs. And while there has never been a single report of the patient making a spontaneous recovery during the waiting time before organ donation, there are cases of 'return of spontaneous circulation' (sometimes known as the Lazarus phenomenon) in patients undergoing resuscitation. Just saying.

It's worth noting that researchers who study people in comas are among the people most keen to write these 'living wills' or 'advance medical directives'. That's because they start to seem like a medical necessity once you have direct line of sight to the thin line between life and death. Comas and their consequences are a very good reason to think hard about death.

How Near To Death Is A Coma?

> I was impressed to find you have a Bacon number of 3.

> What?

> I can link you to Kevin Bacon via a chain of just two other people. Bacon was in *A Few Good Men* with Tom Cruise…

> Go on…

> Cruise was in Valkyrie with Bill Nighy, and Nighy was in *Chalet Girl* with y…

> Stop right there. I thought we agreed never to mention my part in that film again?

First, we should define our terms. A coma patient is completely still and unresponsive, has closed eyes and does not respond to any stimulus. People don't tend to stay in a coma for more than a few weeks; after that, they may die, or recover consciousness, or move towards other states of disturbed consciousness, such as the vegetative state or unresponsive wakefulness syndrome. In that condition, their eyes are open but they will never respond meaningfully to any stimulation. Some of these patients might be able to follow simple commands, like 'look up' or 'move your thumb'. They might look round the room, they will have sleep and wake cycles, and they might even grunt or snore. But because they are still not able to do so consistently and communicate in a meaningful way, they are said to be in a minimally conscious state. Astonishingly, after being unresponsive for decades, even 'persistent' vegetative state patients have been known to regain full consciousness.

Then there's a 'pseudocoma', also known as locked-in syndrome. Here, a patient can't move a muscle, except, sometimes, an eye or eyebrow. Otherwise, they're fine: fully conscious and fully cognizant of what is going on around them. Somewhere within the locked-in category – the definitions are tricky to pick apart, even for professionals – there's the state that neuroscientist Adrian Owen calls 'the Grey Zone'. Here, patients appear to be in a vegetative state but are fully conscious. They are able to hear, see and make sense of the world, but unable to respond to it. In other words, their state of consciousness is higher than patients in a vegetative state, but this is only discovered by means of brain-scanning technology.

Rather chillingly, we only identified the Grey Zone state in 2006, when Owen was using a brain scanner to see if he could see any evidence of awareness in vegetative state patients. Kate Bainbridge had been (supposedly) in such a state since 1997, after a viral infection had put her into a coma. Then along came Owen with his positron-electron tomography (PET) brain scanner. He was showing people in vegetative states photographs of familiar faces to see if any part of their brain responded. Bainbridge's brain 'lit up like a Christmas tree', as he put it. Years later, after lots of innovative communication therapy, Bainbridge made a full recovery and wrote Owen a moving and heartfelt letter describing her gratitude for his brain scans. 'It scares me to think of what might have happened to me if I had not had mine,' she wrote. 'It was like magic, it found me.'

Bainbridge's experience is probably not a rarity – except for the being found bit. Owen reckons that as many as one in five patients diagnosed as being in a 'vegetative state' could be living with a mind that is in full working order. It's tempting to put this down to a near-miraculous recovery, but it's actually more likely that the doctor in charge misdiagnosed the state. It's a scary thought, but we are working towards doing better in diagnosis and communication. Top of the list is giving back some control to patients whose brain scans show activity.

People who have recovered from persistent vegetative states often say that the worst aspect of such states is the lack of self-determination. They obviously don't have much going on in their lives, and so they want to decide simple things, such as which TV channel is on. And that is now becoming possible.

It turns out that a number of locked-in and Grey-Zone patients can train themselves to respond to questions by imagining certain activities. This causes increased blood flow

---

I'm still here

Don't read this if you're going into hospital for an operation any time soon. There's a phenomenon called 'accidental awareness during general anaesthesia'. It's exactly what you think it is: the anaesthetic has made you immobile and unable to breathe for yourself, and you're not meant to even be conscious, let alone able to feel pain. But...

In the UK, the Royal College of Anaesthetists reckons it only happens during something like 1 in 20,000 operations where a general anaesthetic is used, and then usually only for five minutes or fewer. The good news is that only one in five of those who experience accidental awareness feel any pain, and two-thirds of accidentally aware patients don't feel touch or hear sounds; they are simply aware of not being able to move their body. Most people don't wake up knowing it happened: the memory of it resurfaces days later. In the worst cases, it leads to PTSD and depression, but most people who have experienced accidental awareness have no long-lasting effects.

---

to the parts of the brain associated with actually doing that activity. Owen and other researchers have used the two parts of the brain associated with moving limbs and with spatial awareness to set up a kind of binary, yes–no communication system that enables patients to answer questions.

The first time this was done, it sparked a major controversy. A twenty-nine-year-old man learned to imagine playing a tennis stroke for 'yes' and to imagine moving around his home for 'no'. An fMRI scanner showed he could respond correctly to a set of questions about his family. He had been in a vegetative state for almost seven years, since suffering serious brain injuries in a car accident. Family and friends had been talking about whether it was worth keeping him on life support. Suddenly, all that talk had to stop – as did all the other, similar talk around the world. It became immediately clear that we desperately and urgently needed to ask difficult questions about how we care for – or stop caring for – patients who have no easy way to communicate with the outside world. Given what we now know, it's hard to argue that a lack of obvious responsiveness is enough to justify turning off life support.

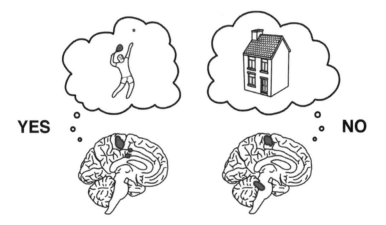

Some vegetative state patients can communicate via the brain activity detected when they imagine playing tennis or navigating around their home

But can we really keep everyone in a permanent vegetative state alive, just in case? The situation is made worse by the fact that there is some controversy around the interpretation of fMRI signals and the appalling revelation that many of us can't, when we imagine playing tennis or moving around the house, produce brain signals big enough to be picked up by the fMRI – even in our fully functioning healthy state. If you're not terribly imaginative, get practising your mental tennis right now.

There are other options. There's a technique similar to fMRI which is called functional near-infrared spectroscopy, and researchers such as Niels Birbaumer at the University of Geneva have used this where other techniques have failed. They tried it on four patients, and by the time they had each answered about 100 questions, the computer could interpret their brain signals for yes and no sufficiently accurately to register their response to the question 'Are you happy?' All four of them said yes.

It's a troubling finding when you consider all the people who have been 'switched off' in the past. How many of them heard the bedside conversations about whether they should be kept alive? How many of them were aware when loved ones had made the decision to move on with their lives? We will never know, but it seems like something we need to think about. Otherwise, history might judge us alongside the people who didn't bother waiting for putrefaction to set in before burying a 'corpse'.

Can I Create A Near-death Experience?

Peter Filardi wrote *Flatliners* after a friend told him about an experience of 'dying' for thirty seconds during an operation.

 Did his friend go down a tunnel of light?

Nope, literally nothing happened. Apparently it was a shockingly dull near-death experience.

Ah, that must be the story that inspired the 2017 remake.

In the opening scenes of *Flatliners*, we see Julia Roberts's character documenting the stories of patients who have had near-death experiences. No wonder she can't resist the opportunity to get involved herself. When you hear about them, they do sound to (almost) die for. People talk about joy, and peace, and walking down a tunnel of light towards long-lost loved ones.

Here's one example, reported in a 1998 paper published in the journal *Medical Psychiatry*. A fifty-five-year-old truck driver who underwent a quadruple heart bypass was able to tell his surgeon about specific things the surgeon did during the operation, because the truck driver was watching the whole thing from above the table. Or that's how he felt. The surgeon agreed that he had done those things, and at the moments the truck driver described. The truck driver also said he saw a brilliant light, which he followed through a tunnel to what he described as a region of warmth, joy and peace, where he met his dead mother and brother-in-law, who told him he must return to his body. According to the paper, the truck driver 'awoke with an intense passion for helping others and desire to talk about his experience, much to the dismay of his embarrassed wife, who belittled what she called his "spook story" and forbade him to mention what he regarded as the focal point of his life'.

Humans have long had such experiences. The Greek writers Heraclitus, Democritus and Plato all wrote about it, describing people who apparently died, then recovered, then told anyone and everyone who would listen about their time in another world. The first scientist to engage with near-death experiences was Sir William Barrett, a physicist who worked at London's Royal Institution and was a Fellow of the Royal Society. However, he was a strong advocate of telepathy, clairvoyance and the idea that the living could talk to the dead, which was enough to make many of his colleagues somewhat sceptical about his ability to dig into these issues with any scientific rigour. Barrett's only real contribution to the field was a 1926 book that told stories of people's near-death encounters. You won't be surprised to hear, given his interests, that Barrett was uncritical of the idea that people were bumping into and engaging with the dead at these moments.

For all the scepticism, as medicine progressed through the twentieth century, reports of near-death experiences became ever more common. The fact that people's bodies were getting closer to shutdown before they were revived meant that more and more people had the conscious journey of hearing themselves declared dead, seeing a long, dark tunnel and being rushed through a review of their major life events.

In 1975, an American doctor called Raymond Moody wrote a book describing all this, and people lapped it up. *Life After Life* was a huge bestseller, prompting sceptical scientists to investigate Moody's claim that this was a universal experience that people had previously been too frightened of mockery to report. What they found was shocking: it turns out that anywhere between 9 and 18 per cent (it depended on the survey) of hospital patients whose lives were in serious danger reported experiences similar to those Moody had described.

They often talked of encountering a 'point of no return' and making an active decision to return to their physical body. Frequently, it was a positive, even euphoric experience.

Floated above your body?

Yes   No

☐   ☐

Walked down a tunnel of light?

Yes   No

☐   ☐

Encountered dead people?

Yes   No

☐   ☐

Sensed overwhelming joy and peace?

Yes   No

☐   ☐

People avoid you at parties?

Yes   No

☐   ☐

If you answer 'yes' to these questions, congratulations — you've had a near-death experience

It sounds like hippy-dippy nonsense, but it's not just hippies who report such happenings. Being religious or spiritual, suffering mental illness or being aware of the stories around near-death experiences, don't make it any more likely that you'll have this experience. For all our scepticism, we have to admit that it is nonetheless 'real'. So what's going on?

Perhaps we should start with the fact that all our experience, even when awake, is a form of hallucination. Our brains only deal in electrical and chemical signals: these are interpreted as sights and sounds and smells in a hugely complex internal representation of the world that is entirely subjective. No one else can experience or access or check this personal view of the world. As neuroscientist Anil Seth has put it, we're all hallucinating all the time, and when we agree about the hallucinations, we call it 'reality'.

It's no surprise, then, that a body in extreme stress might send signals to the brain that change the perception of what's real from the universally agreed version. Psychologists Sue Blackmore and Tom Troscianko have tested this in computer simulations of the output from the visual cortex. They simulated the effect of 'disinhibition' in the neural cells, so that brain activity ran out of control in a manner that is known to happen during oxygen starvation, under the influence of certain drugs or during migraines or seizures. What they found is that this increased noise in the simulated visual cortex produces a field of vision where 'eventually the whole screen is filled with light. The appearance is just like a dark speckly tunnel with a white light at the end, and the light grows bigger and bigger (or nearer and nearer) until it fills the whole screen.'

See what they did there? Blackmore notes that the brain

infers movement from its sensory inputs, and if the visual input is an overwhelming expanding circle of light, that would give the sense of moving through a tunnel towards the light.

It's not hard to imagine that other manifestations of the near-death experience come from other overactive brain circuits. Especially as we know that some of them occur in other situations. As we saw in Chapter 7, sleep disorders can create visual hallucinations and a sense of being outside the body. People with 'walking corpse syndrome', for instance, have the sense that they are dead. It sometimes occurs in patients suffering the advanced stages of multiple sclerosis and typhoid fever, and seems to be associated with abnormal activity in the prefrontal cortex and the parietal cortex. These areas are involved with constructing a coherent reality.

Many hallucinogenic drugs affect the brain in ways that give – surprise! – hallucinations. Many other drugs stimulate euphoria. And if your brain overproduces the neurotransmitter dopamine it can give you visions of meeting other figures; we know this because it's a side effect of treatments for Parkinson's disease, and many sufferers have reported encounters with ghosts and monsters.

In other words, we don't actually need to invoke the existence of celestial beings, another plane of reality or heaven or hell, to explain near-death experiences. That near-spiritual sense is just a manifestation of a brain glitch. It's not unlike déjà vu. It's not unlike déjà vu.*

Nonetheless, a near-death experience can be an extraordinarily positive thing. Many people find it a life-changing moment, after which they have a strong sense of peace and

* Yes, we made this joke in the last book. Which only adds to the brilliance of this one.

purpose, a hugely diminished fear of death and a more confident and outgoing personality. Obviously, you'll want to avoid them at parties, but it's hard not to be at least a little bit happy for them.

Will We Ever Cheat Death?

What do you think you'd encounter in a near-death experience?

Well, I never bullied anyone like Kiefer and Kevin, so probably just good stuff. You?

I wasn't a bully either. But I have mocked a lot of people online.

Your near-death experience is going to be a run-through of your deleted tweets.

In that case, kill me now. Some of those tweets were pure gold.

We saw, when we looked at *Benjamin Button*, that there are many ways we can fight the onslaught of biological degradation that eventually results in death. But, perhaps, instead of fighting by using technologies that halt or undo the problematic processes taking place in our cells, we should just stick two fingers up at death from beyond the grave.

That sounds ridiculous, but there are two ways in which we might do this. In fact, you could embrace one of them right now. Welcome to the strange and extraordinarily optimistic world of cryopreservation.

Remember in Chapter 5 when we talked about the relative difficulties of freezing embryos, sperm and eggs, then thawing them intact so they can fulfil their biological destiny? Well, how about doing the same thing with your head?

If that sounds completely ridiculous, you might have forgotten the Yale project we mentioned on page 250: reviving a four-hour-dead pig brain might be just the first step along this road. That's certainly the attitude shown by all the people whose frozen bodies are already sitting in liquid nitrogen, ready to be thawed when the time comes. That time is not yet here: we don't have the technology to unfreeze without inflicting damage on the cells (nor the technology to repair any damage that does occur). Nevertheless, the owners of these bodies are the pioneering 'transhumanists' who will one day change the human experience of death. Or so they say.

Many of the frozen bodies are (predictably) in California, housed in the facilities of a company called Alcor Life Extension. It's not a bunch of cranks: Aubrey de Grey, who we met in Chapter 9, is one of the names on Alcor's scientific advisory board. The company will freeze your whole body on your death for $200,000 – provided you've also kept up with annual payments (usually a few hundred dollars, max). There's a surcharge to pay if you're outside of the US, though. Alcor reckons that, for best results, your body should be transported to its facilities as quickly as possible after death, and if you're in Europe or China that will be expensive.

It's only $80,000 for Alcor to freeze just your head, by the way. But if you don't have that kind of cash, you could try the Siberian-based KrioRus.* At the moment, their facilities contain the frozen remains of sixty-five people and thirty-one pets. They'll do a whole body for just $36,000, or the equivalent in roubles. 'Finance and payment plans are flexible,' their website says, 'but a lump sum payment when making arrangements and signing up is recommended.'

At the end of 2018, Alcor had 164 'patients' frozen in its storage facilities and more than 1000 people signed up for future freezing. There's lots of obvious questions, such as who will revive the 'patients' and when. Alcor's contract with these people has the answer: 'When, in Alcor's best good faith judgement, it is determined that attempting revival is in the best interests of the Member in cryopreservation, Alcor shall attempt to revive and rehabilitate the Member.'

You've just got to hope that Alcor is still up and running as a going concern at that unspecified date in the future. There is reason for optimism here, though. The Japanese construction company Kongō Gumi was founded in 578 AD. That's more than 1440 years ago. Surely, Alcor can survive until we have the technology to defrost and repair these pioneers?

OK, so we're still sceptical. But for all the ridicule they endure, their hopes are not entirely without foundation. Bacteria can survive freezing – in 2007, researchers managed to revive some that had been frozen into Arctic ice eight million years ago. And then there's the wood frog, an amphibian that routinely survives almost half of its body freezing. Ice

---

* We think this is a Russian-language contraction of 'cryogenics' and 'Russia', but we're not averse to the idea that it's actually based on Toys R Us.

crystals form under the frog's skin, its heart stops beating and it doesn't breathe. It would seem, by medieval standards at least, to be dead. But for as long as eleven days it can come back to life.

This is possible because the frog's body contains proteins and glucose molecules that have evolved to stop the cells themselves bursting open at such low temperatures. And we are starting to be able to perform the same trick.

No one has done it on humans yet, but researchers at a company called 21st Century Medicine have done it on rabbit brains. First, they drained the blood from the brains, then replaced it with a chemical called glutaraldehyde, which can be cooled without expanding in the potentially cell-bursting way that water-based fluids always will. They cooled the rabbit brains to -135°C, then brought them back up to room temperature a week later. All the connections between the rabbit's neurons were intact, suggesting that – if the rabbit had actually been alive throughout the initial procedure – it might have had a functioning brain when thawed, and perhaps all its memories and learned behaviours too. And so, their argument goes, preserving people with memories and personality intact might be possible.

That's a huge leap, obviously. Yes, we've frozen and thawed worms and seen them exhibit behaviours they had learned before they experienced the cold snap. But worms, rabbits and people are all very different. Also, glutaraldehyde is highly toxic – you possibly wouldn't expect a human being to survive being pickled in a toxic chemical before being flash-frozen and defrosted centuries later.

Perhaps, then, the second option for eternal life is a better bet. Here, we're not limited by biology. Instead we become silicon-based beings: all we have to do is upload our minds.

> ### See also
>
> There is no shortage of films about life after death, but life after near-death – or something like it – is a little more niche. Best known, perhaps, is the triple-Oscar-nominated *Awakenings*, based on Oliver Sacks' book about patients who recover from encephalitis after decades in a catatonic state. The film stars Robin Williams and Robert De Niro, and is a good watch. Then there's Ricky Gervais in *Ghost Town*. Here, he plays a version of himself (obviously) who has a near-death experience that results in him being able to see ghosts. 1998's *Eden* is the story of a woman with multiple sclerosis who has out-of-body experiences at night, and eventually falls into a coma. It's pretty melodramatic but it was nominated for the Grand Jury Prize at the 1996 Sundance Film Festival, so what do we know?

Admittedly, this one's a stretch too. The idea is straightforward enough: you create a perfect copy of all the connections in your brain, together with the information they encode, in a computer. That computer now hosts a copy of You. Philosophically, though, it's a bit of a nightmare. Are we sure that our selves are so neatly contained within our brain's structure? Are we able to capture all the essentials or will there be missing information that creates nothing more than a cheap facsimile of our rich inner lives? When do we upload, if we do it too soon will there actually be two of us? And how can we even think of doing this when we don't know anything about what consciousness is or how it works?

Despite all this, there's already a start-up that's working on the idea. Nectome aren't doing the uploading yet: they're just preserving the brain, ready for analysis and uploading once that side of the equation is up and running. The problem is, they need a fresh brain to work on, so their ideal customer is someone with a fatal disease who is willing to undergo euthanasia in their embalming facilities. Apparently, this is all entirely legal where Nectome is based: in (you guessed it) California.

It sounds ludicrous, doesn't it? But don't scoff too soon. A couple of dozen people have signed up already, paying a $10,000 deposit (fully refundable if they change their biological minds) to go on the waiting list for when the technology is ready. Not all scientists have said their goal is entirely impossible (though the least pessimistic quote might be from Ken Hayworth of the Howard Hughes Medical Institute, who told *STAT News*, 'I think the chances that brain preservation will result in future revival are slim but not zero.').

Are you in?

ACKNOWLEDGEMENTS

Right then. Who are we thanking this time round?

Firstly, all of the experts who have spoken to us on the *Science(ish)* podcast or checked over our words, or both – Toby Walsh, Jonathan Quick, Aubrey de Grey, Shanna Swan, Monica Gagliano, Pete Feaver, Henry Nicholls, Megan Bruck Syal, David Keith and Leslie Whetstein. Without them, we'd be really struggling.

Speak for yourself. I'd like to thank my mum and dad for doing a wonderful job.

A wonderful job of what? Recognizing their error and not having any more kids after you?

Well, recognizing that they weren't going to be able to improve.

And leaving me to work with a classic Only Child. Thanks Patricia. Thanks Philip.

I want to add that our illustrator Colin Kersley has done such great stuff that I'm worried it's making the words look bad.

I'm not sure we can blame the pictures for that.

Can we blame our editor Mike Harpley? Again?

I think that would be unfair. He deserves a lot of credit for his patience with our casual attitude towards 'deadlines' and 'printing schedules' and 'word count'.

Oh, and the Radio Wolfgang crew aren't going to thank themselves. Our whip-smart producers Eli Block, Elle Scott and Cormac Macauliffe; Ivor 'Slayer' Manley on sound for his constant slaying. Colm Roche for letting us keep on making the podcast even though it makes no financial sense whatsoever.

That reminds me, I'm very grateful to my agent Patrick Walsh who continues to represent me even though it makes no financial sense whatsoever.

I obviously have to shout out to my ideal wife Emer, who has put up with yet more of me sitting in sullen silence and then occasionally bellowing things like 'Did you know that a plant has eaten a rat?' at her.

Hard to know whose wife has a tougher time. But probably yours.

Is that it?

Not quite. I'd like to thank you for always making me look clever.

I'm taking that as a compliment even though I know it wasn't.

Index

Samsung SGR-A1 (gun), 98
Santomauro, Julia, 169
SARS (severe acute respiratory syndrome), 20
satellites, 133, 136–9
Saturn, 35
Schelling, Thomas, 232
Schiff, Richard, 132
Schumacher, Joel, 246
Schwarzenegger, Arnold, 81–2, 92–3
Science of Sleep, The, 171
SCoPEx (Stratospheric Controlled Perturbation Experiment), 131, 133
Secret Life of Plants, The (Tompkins & Bird), 176
senescence, *see* ageing
'senolytics', 210–11, 213
senomodifiers, 213
SENS (Strategies for Engineered Negligible Senescence), 216–17
SenseTime, 95
Seth, Anil, 262
sharks, 69–77
  fishing, 72
  goblin sharks, 74
  great whites, 70
  shark attacks, 76–7, 79
Shyamalan, M. Night, 196
Siberia, Russia, 48, 140
Singapore, 116
Sirtris, 213
SIV (simian immunodeficiency virus), 12
Slayman, Clifford, 176
sleep, 151–72, 263
  cataplexy, 167
  insomnia, 151–2, 157–60, 169–71
  narcolepsy, 167–8
  paralysis, 168–70
  rapid eye movement (REM), 160, 162–3
  sexsomnia, 165
  sleepwalking, 164–5
  trackers, 172
  'walking corpse syndrome', 263
smoking, 149–50

Society for Plant Neurobiology, 176–7
Society of Plant Signaling and Behavior, 177
Solar and Heliospheric Observatory (SOHO), 137
solar system, 35–7
South Africa, 189
South China Morning Post, 142
South Korea, 240
Soviet Union, 136, 225, 228, 233
  see also Russia
SpaceX, 132
Spanish flu, *see* influenza
sperm, 106, 110–11, 113–14, 118, 121–3, 125, 160
spherules, 46–7
Spielberg, Steven, 57–8, 75, 238
Spot (robot), 86
SpotMini (robot), 87
Sputnik, 136
St Lucia, 169
Stanford University, 123, 131
Star Wars program, 138
Starfish Prime (nuclear bomb), 53
STAT News, 269
Statham, Jason, 78
stem cells, 121, 125, 214–15
Steptoe, Patrick, 117, 123
Still Alice, 219
storms, 143–50
Strategy of Conflict, The (Schelling), 232
Strychnos nux-vomica, 182
Stuxnet, 235–6
'super-spreaders', 20–21
'supercentenarians', 208
Sutherland, Kiefer, 246–7
Swan, Shanna, 106, 110, 113
Switzerland, 239

'Taung Child', 65
telomeres, 218
Tempel 1 (comet), 42
Terminator films, 81–3, 88, 90–91, 97, 98
Tesla, 95